The Effects of L1 and L2 Use in the L2 Classroom

第二言語指導における学習者母語活用の可能性

松本 祐子（Yuko Matsumoto）

UNIVERSITY EDUCATION PRESS

は じ め に

　本論文は 2016 年度津田塾大学文学研究科（コミュニケーション研究英語教育専攻）に提出された学位論文である。2011 年 4 月より約 5 年間、同研究科後期博士課程において取りくんだ研究の成果をまとめた。以下に研究の経緯と本書の構成を簡単に述べる。

　近年日本の英語教育では「英語は英語で」指導するというアプローチが奨励されている。高等学校では既に 2013 年度から実施されており、中学校でも 2020 年度からこのアプローチが採用される。しかしながらその導入に際し、第二言語習得理論の観点からも、学習者や教師の立場を考慮した実践的観点からも十分な議論が尽くされているとは言い難い。筆者は「オールイングリッシュアプローチ」を採用する大学での授業に 10 年以上携わってきたが、その可能性と共に様々な課題も実感している。そこで使用言語が英語学習に与える影響を探るため、本研究を行った。研究の概要は「論文要旨」に譲るが、本研究が今後の英語指導において、柔軟性のある効果的な言語使用のあり方を示す一助となることを願う。

　本論文は様式規定に基づき "Abstract, Acknowledgement, Table of Contents, Chapter I – V, References, and Appendices" という構成である。本書の冒頭に論文の要旨をまとめた "Summary"（英文）と「論文要旨」（和文）を合わせて掲載した。

　本書の出版は津田塾大学「鷲見八重子出版奨励金」を受けて実現した。鷲見先生のご厚意に深く感謝申し上げたい。この感謝を胸に刻み、今後も英語教育の実践と研究に取り組んでいきたいと考える。大学創設者である津田梅子が女子英語教育のために放った "Guiding light" は 100 年の時を経てなお、静かに輝き続けている。

2017 年 5 月

松本祐子

Summary

This paper investigates the effects of language use during peer interaction on reading comprehension and reading attitudes in the English classroom. It has been long debated whether students' first language (L1) should be allowed or excluded in the second language (L2) classroom. The current trend of English education in Japan has been oriented toward an "English-only" approach. That is, teachers and students are strongly encouraged to use English for instruction and production regardless of the proficiency level, the content of a lesson, or the purpose of a class. At the same time, the trend is toward eliminating students' L1 (Japanese), which is considered as an obstacle for L2 learning. Yet research to date in the field of second language acquisition (SLA) has not proven the clear superiority of exclusive L2 use for teaching or learning. In fact, various researchers have pointed out the benefits of partial L1 use during the L2 lesson as a means of providing students with pedagogical and affective support. For instance, the L1 can be effectively used by students for regulating cognitive processes, enhancing vocabulary learning, raising the quality of L2 output, enabling higher-level text comprehension, and promoting collaboration. When it is used by the teacher, the L1 is beneficial for increasing efficiency and accuracy of instruction as well as for building rapport and maintaining discipline.

Considering such practical benefits of L1 support in the L2 classroom, it seems rather inflexible to insist on eliminating the use of the L1 in favor of only providing instructions via the L2. Instead, it would be more logical to seek effective ways to partially use the L1 as a support for promoting L2 learning, in light of empirical research as well as SLA theories. The current study, which has been designed with that purpose in mind, pursues two goals in particular. The first goal is to examine the effect of students' "language use in either the L1 or L2" (henceforth referred to simply as "language use") during peer interaction on L2 learning and reading. The second goal is to theoretically and empirically present effective ways of language use in the L2 classroom, drawing on theoretical support that includes Cummins' (2001) concept of "common underlying proficiency," "multi-competence" proposed by V. Cook (2008), and the changing roles of English from a sociolinguistic perspective. Furthermore, in order to specify the circumstances of the L1 and L2 use, this paper's literature review examines the levels and settings of reading as well as the influential factors for L2 reading. The researcher hopes that the suggested models of language use will pave the way for a new teaching approach that can optimize the L1 use to promote L2 learning.

The current study conducted an experiment focusing on Japanese university students, who consisted of two cohorts: upper-intermediate and novice levels. Each cohort was divided into two groups: one group that engaged in pair work in the L1 (Japanese) and the other that conducted the pair work in the L2 (English). The procedure of the experiment was as follows. First, the participants read a short reading passage (a newspaper editorial) individually without consulting a dictionary. Second, after the reading text was removed, a buffer task was conducted, through which the participants provided information regarding their English learning experiences, their evaluation of text difficulty, and their background knowledge about the topic of the text. Third, the participants engaged in pair work to discuss seven focus questions intended to have them recall essential information about the text. As described above, for each level, half of the participants did L1 pair work and the other half did L2 pair work. Fourth, the participants took a text-removed summary completion test individually. Fifth, the participants answered the post-research questionnaire. Finally, one week after the class, the participants took a delayed summary completion test without consulting the reading text or a dictionary. The data obtained was analyzed statistically via a two-way mixed analysis of variance (ANOVA), t-test, and Pearson's chi-square. Some of the data was also analyzed descriptively. The purpose of this data analysis is to answer the following five research questions that the current study has presented:

1. Does the "language use either in the L1 or L2" (henceforth referred to simply as "language use") during the pair work influence the results of the summary completion test and the delayed summary completion test; and does this influence vary depending on the English proficiency levels?

2. Does the language use during the pair work influence the pair-work production; and does this influence vary depending on the English proficiency levels?

3. Does the language use during the pair work influence the numerical and survey evaluation of the pair work; and does this influence vary depending on the English proficiency levels?

4. Does the language use during the pair work influence pair-work language preference and the survey evaluation; and does this influence vary depending on the English proficiency levels?

5. Do the different circumstances of the reading lesson influence the participants' language preference, L1 or L2?

The results of the current study are summarized as follows according to each research question (RQ). RQ (1) explored the influence of pair-work language use on L2 reading comprehension. The study has found that for both proficiency levels (upper-intermediate and novice), there was no significant difference between the L1 and L2 pair-work groups in terms of participants' performance on the summary completion test or delayed summary completion test at statistically significant level. RQ (2) examined the results of pair work (i.e., scores of focus questions), which showed that the L1 pair-work groups significantly surpassed the L2 pair-work groups at both the upper-intermediate and novice levels. In addition, the elicited audio-recorded pair work (four pairs in each L1 and L2 pair-work group at each level: total 16 pairs' recording) indicated that L1 pairs in general had more active peer interaction (e.g., equal contribution between the participants, more turn-takings). This clearly suggests that the L1 pair work was beneficial for promoting peer interaction and enhancing the quality of pair-work production. RQ (3) explored the evaluation of the pair work by the L1 and L2 pair-work groups at each level. Both L1 and L2 groups at the upper-intermediate level valued the pair work positively and there was no significant difference between the groups. The novice level, on the other hand, showed a significant difference between the two groups. That is, the L1 group valued the pair work significantly more than the L2 group. These results indicate that the L1 pair work was beneficial for the novice participants, and that this benefit is clearly recognized by the participants. With regard to RQ (4), the preference of pair-work language (L1 preference, L2 preference, or no preference) was significantly different between the L1 and L2 groups at the upper-intermediate level. That is, the preference by the L2 pair-work group split evenly among the three categories, whereas the vast majority of the L1 pair-work group showed an L1 preference. The novice level, on the other hand, did not indicate any significant difference between the L1 and L2 pair-work groups. The majority of them showed an L1 preference. Finally RQ (5) examined the participants' language preference in eight different circumstances during the reading lesson. The results showed that the L1 is preferred when the participants want to precisely understand the content of given information, such as when the teacher is explaining grammar rules or structures; providing answers of reading comprehension questions, or making classroom announcements. The L2 is preferred, on the other hand, when certain patterns of interaction can be expected, such as when the teacher is providing the answers to reading comprehension questions or asking questions. These results indicate that participants' language preference significantly varies according to the circumstances of the lesson.

As for the first goal of the current study, which is to examine the effects of peer-interaction language use on L2 reading and reading attitudes, the researcher has confirmed the following five points as conclusions. First, it is possible to use either the L1 or L2 flexibly during pair work for reading comprehension after carefully considering learners' proficiency level and the purpose of the lesson. Second, L1 use is beneficial to pair-work production, both quantitatively and qualitatively, regardless of proficiency levels. Third, the novice learners tend to appreciate L1 pair work much more than L2 pair work. Fourth, the upper-intermediate level seems capable of conducting L2 pair work if necessary, while the novice level seems to have difficulty in taking part in L2 pair work effectively unless sufficient support is provided. Finally, as the fifth conclusion, appropriate language use appears to change according to the circumstances of the lesson.

With regard to the other goal of this paper, which is to theoretically and empirically present effective ways of partially using the L1 to promote L2 learning, the researcher has suggested three models

viii

associated with (a) a twofold focus of L2 learning/teaching, (b) the process of the L2 lesson, and (c) the learners' proficiency level and conditions of the lesson.

Although further research is needed to more clearly identify types of effective language use in the L2 classroom, this paper has been able to meet the two main research goals described above.

論文要旨

　この論文は、英語クラスのピアインタラクションで使用される言語が英文読解や読解態度にどのような影響を与えうるかを探るものである。第二言語指導において学習者の第一言語を使用するか、あるいは排除するかは長い間議論されてきた。日本の英語教育の潮流は近年「イングリッシュ・オンリー」アプローチの方向に向かいつつある。つまり、学習者の英語力、レッスンの内容、あるいはクラスの目的に関わらず、教師の指導及び学習者の発話は英語で行うことが強く奨励されている。この一方で学習者の第一言語（日本語）は、第二言語（英語）学習の妨げになるものとして排除されつつある。しかしながら第二言語習得研究の分野において、排他的な第二言語使用がその指導や学習に明らかに効果的であるとは未だ証明されていない。実際は様々な研究者が、実践的及び心理的なサポートを与えうるという理由から、第二言語指導における部分的な第一言語使用の利点を指摘している。例えば、学習者が第一言語を使用することにより認知的なプロセスを統制したり、語彙学習の効果を上げたり、発話の質を高めたり、より高度なレベルのテキストに取り組むことを可能にしたり、学習者同士の協同を促進したりすることが可能になる。一方で教師が第一言語を使用する場合、第二言語のみで行うよりも指導の効率や正確性を高めるだけでなく、学習者との信頼関係を築き教室内の規律を保つことにも効果的であるとされる。

　このように教室における第一言語使用の利点を考えるとき「英語のみによる指導及び日本語の排除」という方針はやや柔軟性に欠けると言わざるを得ない。むしろ実践的リサーチや第二言語習得理論に基き、第二言語学習を促進するためにはどのように第一言語を利用するのが効果的かを探る方が理にかなっている。本研究はこれを大きな目標とし、以下2つのポイントに研究の焦点

を当てる。まず使用言語が第二言語学習にどのような影響を与えるかを調べるために実験を行う。具体的には、異なる言語を使用したピアインタラクションと読解や読解態度との関係を調べる。次に文献研究を基軸に、第二言語学習を促進するための第一言語活用の方法を理論的・実践的視点から考察する。特に理論的サポートとしてCummins（2001）の共有基底言語能力（common underlying proficiency）、V. Cook（2008）が提唱するマルチコンピテンス（multicompetence）、及び変化する英語の役割に関する社会言語学的見地の3点を取り上げる。更に第一言語と第二言語使用の場面を特定するために、読みのレベルや読解活動の設定条件、及び第二言語読解に影響を与える要因等について文献研究で論じる。最後に第二言語学習の促進を目的とした効果的な言語使用モデルを提案する。

　本研究は日本人大学習者を対象とした実験を行った。学習者は中上級レベルと初級レベルの2集団からなる。更にそれぞれの集団はペアワークで使用する言語により第一言語（日本語）グループと第二言語（英語）グループに分類された。実験の手順は以下の通りである。まず学習者は辞書を使わずに短い英文テキスト（約400字の新聞社説記事）を個別に読む。テキストが回収された後、次にバッファタスクが配布され、英語学習経験、読解テキストの難易度、読解テキストのトピックに関する背景知識に関して回答を行う。続くペアワークでは、読解テキストの主要情報を問う7つのフォーカス・クエスチョンについて指定された言語で話し合いと記述回答を行う。これはテキストの重要な情報を記憶から抽出させることを目的としている。先に述べたように各レベル集団の半数は日本語ペアワークを、のこりの半数は英語ペアワークを行う。次に学習者はテキストを見ないで、選択式穴埋めサマリーテストを個別に受ける。最後に学習者は事後質問票調査に回答する。1週間後、辞書やテキストを参照することなく、学習者は遅延選択式穴埋めサマリーテストを受ける。収集データは二要因分散分析（混合計画）、t検定、カイ二乗検定によって統計分析された。それ以外のデータは記述的分析が行われた。これらの分析は以下5つのリサーチクエスチョンに答えるために実施された。

1. ペアワーク中の使用言語（日本語または英語）は選択式穴埋めサマリーテストや遅延選択式穴埋めサマリーテストの結果に影響を与えるか？　またその影響は英語能力レベルごとに異なるか？
2. ペアワーク中の使用言語はペアワークの成果に影響を与えるか？　またその影響は英語能力レベルごとに異なるか？
3. ペアワーク中の使用言語はペアワークの数値的及び記述的評価に影響を与えるか？　またその影響は英語能力レベルごとに異なるか？
4. ペアワーク中の使用言語はペアワークで使用を希望する言語の選択に影響を与えるか？　またその影響は英語能力レベルごとに異なるか？
5. リーディング授業内の場面が異なれば、使用を希望する言語も異なるか？

　本研究の結果はリサーチクエスチョン（RQ）ごとに以下のようにまとめられる。まずRQ（1）に関して、ペアワーク時の使用言語（日本語または英語）は、レベルに関わらず、選択式穴埋めサマリーテストや遅延選択式穴埋めサマリーテストの結果に統計的に有意なレベルでは影響を与えなかった。RQ（2）ではペアワークの成果を検証したが、中上級と初級レベル両方において、日本語使用グループの方が有意に良い成績を示した。更に無作為抽出されたペアワークの録音（［日本語グループ4組＋英語グループ4組］×2つのレベル集団＝計16組）により、特に初級レベルにおいて日本語グループの方がより活発にペアワークを行っていることが分かった（例：ペア同士ほぼ対等なタスクへの貢献、より頻繁な発話のやり取り）。これらの結果は、第一言語によるペアワークはピアインタラクションを促進し、ペアワークの成果を高める効果があることを示している。RQ（3）では日本語グループと英語グループがそれぞれどのようにペアワークを評価するかを探った。中上級レベルでは日本語・英語使用グループ共にペアワークを肯定的に評価しており、グループ間に有意な差は見られなかった。一方初級レベルでは、グループ間に有意な違いが見られた。日本語グループの方が英語グループよりも有意に高くペアワークを評価していたのである。これにより初級レベルにとって日本語を使用したペアワークは有益であり、学習者自身もそれを明らかに実感していたことが分かる。言

い換えれば、初級レベルにおいて英語のペアワークは日本語ペアワークほど評価されなかったということになる。RQ（4）ではペアワーク時の使用希望言語（三択：日本語希望、英語希望、どちらでも変わりない）を調査したが、中上級レベルにおいてその回答比率が日本語と英語グループ間で有意に異なることが明らかになった。中上級レベルの英語グループでは上記3つの回答がほぼ等しく選ばれたが、日本語グループでは大多数が日本語希望を示した。一方初級レベルでは日本語・英語グループ間に有意差は見られず、両グループの過半数が日本語使用を希望していた。特に英語グループでは日本語使用を希望する割合が100%であったことは注目に値する。最後にRQ（5）ではリーディングクラス内の8つの異なる場面で使用希望言語がどのように変わるかを調べた。日本語使用を希望するのは学習者が情報の内容を理解したい場面、例えば教師が文法や構文について説明している時、読解問題の解答説明をしている時、連絡事項を伝達している時である。一方英語使用を希望するのは、やり取りのパターンがある程度決まっているような場面、例えば教師が読解問題の答えあわせをしている時や学習者に対して質問をしている時である。これらの結果により、授業の場面ごとに学習者が使用を希望する言語が異なることが分かった。

　本研究の目的のひとつとして、ピアインタラクション時の使用言語が読解や読解の態度に与える影響を調べることを先に掲げた。この点に関して以下5つの発見があった。第一に学習者のレベルやレッスンの目的などを充分考慮した上で、読解のためのペアワークでは第一言語と第二言語どちらも柔軟に使うことができるということが示された。第二に第一言語の使用は、学習者のレベルに関わらず、ペアワークの成果を量的・質的両面において高める効果があるという点が明らかになった。第三に初級レベルでは第一言語を使用したペアワークの方が第二言語を使用したペアワークよりも有意に高く評価されることが分かった。第四に中上級レベルは必要に応じてL2ペアワークを行う言語的能力があるが、初級レベルでは充分なサポートが与えられない限りL2ペアワークを効果的に行うのは難しいということが示された。最後に授業内の場面によって学習者が使用を希望する言語は有意に異なるということも明らかになった。

　本研究のもうひとつの目的は、第二言語学習を促進することを目的とした部

分的第一言語使用のモデルを、理論的・実践的論拠に基づき提案することであった。これに関しては以下３つの焦点と関連付けてそれぞれモデルを提示した。すなわち（a）第二言語学習と指導における２つのフォーカス、（b）第二言語授業のプロセス、（c）学習者のレベルと授業の設定状況である。（a）に関してはLittlewood（2004）の提唱するモデルを参考に、第二言語学習を「分析的活動」と「経験的活動」に分類し、それぞれに適した言語使用のバランスを考察した。（b）については一般的なリーディングクラスの流れ（活動）に沿って、どのように英語と日本語を使い分けていくのが効果的かを提案した。（c）では学習者のレベルや授業の場面（リサーチクエスチョン５参照）、それぞれの読解活動が目指す読みのレベル（Coté, Goldman, and Saul, 1998）、更には文脈に埋め込まれたヒントや認知的負荷の度合いによって変化するタスクの設定状況（Cummins, 2001）などを考慮した言語使用の在り方を統合的に示した。

　今後更に第二言語教室における効果的な言語使用について研究を継続していくことが不可欠だが、先に掲げた２つの目的に関しては本研究である程度達成できたと考える。

Abstract

This paper investigates the effects of language use during peer interaction in the form of pair work on reading comprehension and reading attitudes in the English classroom. Given the various benefits of students' first language (L1) use for the second language (L2) learning and teaching, classroom learning is likely to be enhanced through effective language use, i.e., either in L1 or L2. The current study has conducted an experiment in which Japanese university students (at both the upper-intermediate and novice levels) read a short English passage and engage in pair work either in Japanese (L1) or in English (L2) to discuss the text-related focus questions. The influence of pair-work language use on L2 reading comprehension was gauged using a summary completion test and a delayed summary completion test. The post-research questionnaire examined participants' reading attitudes, such as the evaluation of pair work, the language preference for pair work, and the language preference for different circumstances in the reading lesson.

The results suggest the following five points. First, there was no significant difference between the L1 and L2 pair work in terms of participants' L2 reading comprehension at either the upper-intermediate or novice level. Second, the L1 pair work was beneficial by enhancing the quantity and quality of pair work at both levels. Third, the pair work was valued most by the L1 pair-work group at the novice level. Fourth, the upper-intermediate level L2 pair-work group showed a significantly different pattern of pair-work language preference from the other groups.

Fifth, and finally, language preference varied according to the different circumstances of the reading lesson.

According to the study results and literature review, this paper has also presented three models of effective language use in either the L1 or L2 in association with: (a) a twofold focus of L2 learning and teaching; (b) the process of the L2 lesson; and (c) learners' proficiency level and conditions of the lesson.

Keywords: L1 use, L2 reading comprehension, pair work

Acknowledgements

I would like to express the deepest gratitude to my advisor, Professor Hiroko Tajika, who gave me the opportunity to study in the graduate program at Tsuda University. Without her guidance and untiring assistance, this dissertation would not have been possible. I am also extremely grateful to Professor Mariko Yoshida, Professor Yoshinori Inagaki, Professor Saeko Noda, and Professor Natsumi Okuwaki for the generous support they provided for me as dissertation committee members.

Let me take this opportunity to express my appreciation to all of the other teachers whose careers and scholarship inspired and guided me as I pursued research in the field of English education. I also would like to warmly thank all of the students whom I have encountered over the course of my own teaching career and my fellow classmates and friends at Tsuda University for all of the encouragement and knowledge I have gained from them.

Finally, I would like to thank my parents, Masao and Yumiko Matsumoto, for providing the moral support and practical assistance that allowed me to complete this dissertation, and my husband, Michael, and daughters, Emma and Mia, for their patient support over the past five years.

This dissertation is dedicated to the memory of my late brother, Takuro, who lived his life with great dignity and kindness.

Table of Contents

はじめに ……………………………………………………… *i*

Summary …………………………………………………… *iii*

論文要旨 …………………………………………………… *ix*

Abstract …………………………………………………… *xv*

Acknowledgements ………………………………………… *xvii*

Table of Contents ………………………………………… *xix*

List of Tables ……………………………………………… *xxiii*

List of Figures …………………………………………… *xxiv*

List of Appendices ………………………………………… *xxvi*

Chapter I   Introduction ……………………………… *1*

  A. Statement of the Problem   *1*

  B. Purpose of the Study   *7*

    1. Focus   *7*

    2. Goal   *9*

Chapter II   Literature Review ……………………… *11*

  A. Language Use in the L2 Classroom   *12*

    1. Background of L1 use for language instruction and learning   *12*

      a. Methodological perspectives: To use or not to use   *12*

      b. Empirical research on L1 use in the English classrooms   *16*

    2. Theoretical support for L1 use   *18*

      a. Common underlying proficiency   *18*

      b. Multi-competence   *20*

      c. Sociolinguistic perspectives: Changing roles of English   *22*

3. Pedagogical support for L1 use   *25*

   a. Advantages of L1 use by students   *25*

      i. Regulating cognitive process   *26*

      ii. Enhancing vocabulary learning   *27*

      iii. Increasing quality of L2 output   *30*

      iv. Enabling higher-level text comprehension   *31*

      v. Promoting collaboration   *33*

   b. Advantages of L1 use by the teacher   *35*

      i. Efficiency   *35*

      ii. Accuracy   *35*

      iii. Building rapport and maintaining discipline   *36*

B. Effects of Language Use on L2 Reading   *38*

  1. Mechanism of reading: Two reading models   *39*

  2. Distinctive features of L2 reading   *42*

  3. Circumstances of L1 and L2 use for L2 reading   *44*

   a. Levels of reading: Quality of textbase and degree of background knowledge use   *45*

   b. Settings of reading: Contextual clue and cognitive load   *47*

   c. Influential factors for L2 reading: L2 language ability and L1 reading ability   *50*

C. Effects of Language Use on Peer Interaction   *52*

  1. Effects of peer interaction on L2 learning   *52*

  2. Effects of peer interaction on L2 reading   *54*

D. Hypotheses on the Effects of Language Use during Peer Interaction on L2 Reading   *56*

  1. Summary of literature review   *56*

  2. Summary of previous research (Matsumoto, 2013)   *57*

  3. Hypotheses   *59*

E. Research Questions   *60*

Table of Contents *xxi*

Chapter III The Study ·· *63*

A. Methods   *65*

  1. Participants   *65*

  2. Data collection instruments   *67*

    a. Text-removed summary completion test (ST) and delayed summary completion test (DST) (Appendices E & F)   *68*

    b. Buffer task (BT) (Appendix G)   *69*

    c. Pair work (PW) focus questions (Appendix H)   *70*

    d. Post-research questionnaire (PRSQ) (Appendix J)   *71*

  3. Experimental procedures   *74*

  4. Data analysis tools   *76*

  5. Pilot study   *77*

B. Results   *77*

  1. Research Question (1):

    Influence of language use on reading comprehension   *77*

  2. Research Question (2):

    Influence of language use on the outcomes of pair work   *80*

  3. Research Question (3):

    Influence of language use on pair-work evaluation   *81*

  4. Research Question (4):

    Influence of language use on language preference for pair work   *88*

  5. Research Question (5):

    Language preference in different circumstances during a reading lesson   *96*

Chapter IV   Discussion ······································· *101*

A. Responses to Research Questions   *101*

  1. Research Question (1):

    Influence of language use on reading comprehension   *101*

xxii

2. Research Question (2) :

Influence of language use on the outcomes of pair work   *103*

3. Research Question (3):

Influence of language use on pair-work evaluation   *114*

4. Research Question (4):

Influence of language use on language preference for pair work   *117*

5. Research Question (5):

Language preference in different circumstances during a reading lesson

120

6. Summary   *120*

B. Pedagogical Implications   *122*

1. Language use and a twofold focus of L2 learning and teaching   *123*

2. Language use in the process of L2 lesson   *129*

3. Language use adapted for proficiency levels and circumstances of the lesson   *131*

C. Limitations   *135*

D. Future Research   *136*

Chapter V   Conclusion ·· *139*

References ·· *143*

Appendices ··· *151* *xxiii*

List of Tables

Table

1. Research Design of the Current Study   *64*

2. The Participants   *66*

3. Six Steps of Experimental Procedure   *74*

4. Descriptive Statistics and Two-way Mixed ANOVA Summary Tables on ST and DST   *79*

5. Descriptive Statistics and Two-way Mixed ANOVA Summary Tables on ST and DST   *80*

6. Descriptive Statistics and t-test Summary Tables on PW   *81*

7. Descriptive Statistics and t-test Summary Tables on Numerical PW Evaluation   *83*

8. Descriptive Statistics and Chi-square Test Summary Table for PRSQ (3)   *89*

9. Descriptive Statistics and Chi-square Test Summary Table for PRSQ (5)   *97*

10. Descriptive Statistics and t-test Summary Tables on Turn-taking during PW   *105*

List of Figures

Figure

1. L1 and TL (L2) use in each teaching method and approach   *15*

2. Dual iceberg representation of bilingual proficiency   *19*

3. Four levels of mental representations of a text in line with the quality of textbase and the degree of prior knowledge use   *45*

4. Four settings of a task with consideration to the range of contextual support and the degree of cognitive involvement   *48*

5. Influential factors of L2 reading comprehension   *51*

6. Results of pair-work evaluation for upper-intermediate level   *84*

7. Results of pair-work evaluation for novice level   *84*

8. Positive pair-work survey evaluation by the L1 and L2 pair-work groups for upper-intermediate and novice levels   *86*

9. Negative pair-work survey evaluation by the L1 and L2 pair-work groups for upper-intermediate and novice levels   *87*

10. Percentage of pair-work language preference in L1 and L2 pair-work groups within the upper-intermediate level   *90*

11. Percentage of pair-work language preference in L1 and L2 pair-work groups within the novice level   *91*

12. Reasons of L1 preference chosen by the upper-intermediate level L1 pair-work group   *91*

13. Reasons of L1 preference chosen by the upper-intermediate level L2 pair-work group   *92*

14. Reasons of L2 preference chosen by the upper-intermediate level L2 pair-work group   *93*

15. Reasons of no preference chosen by the upper-intermediate level L2

pair-work group   *94*

16. Reasons of L1 preference chosen by the novice level L1 pair-work group   *94*

17. Reasons of L1 preference chosen by the novice level L2 pair-work group   *95*

18. Continuum from analytical activities to experimental activities

125

19. Sample L1 and L2 use during a reading lesson   *130*

20. Amount of L1 and L2 use during the L2 reading lesson in association with students' proficiency levels, circumstances of the lesson, reading levels, and settings of reading tasks   *133*

xxvi

List of Appendices

Appendix

    A. Previous Research   *151*

    B. Informed Consent   *153*

    C. Taylor's Research on Reading Summary   *154*

    D. Reading Text   *156*

    E. Summary Completion Test   *159*

    F. Delayed Summary Completion Test   *162*

    G. Buffer Task   *165*

    H. Pair Work Focus Questions   *166*

    I. Answer Key for the Pair Work Focus Questions (FQs)   *174*

    J. Post-research Questionnaire   *175*

    K. Pilot Study   *177*

The Effects of L1 and L2 Use in the L2 Classroom
第二言語指導における学習者母語活用の可能性

Chapter I

Introduction

A. Statement of the Problem

It has been long debated whether students' first language (L1) should be allowed or excluded in the second language (L2) classroom. Although quite a few researchers have pointed out the benefits of students' L1 use in supporting L2 learning cognitively and affectively (Butzkamm, 2003; G. Cook, 2010; V. Cook, 2008; Cummins, 2007), the current trend of English (L2) education in Japan seems to rely heavily on the assumption that students' L2 learning would be greatly enhanced by increasing the amount of L2 use and excluding students' L1 (Japanese) as much as possible.

This trend is reflected in the new teaching guidelines for high schools issued by the Ministry of Education, Culture, Sports, Science and Technology (MEXT, 2009), and implemented in April, 2013. The guidelines suggest that high school English lessons, in principle, should be conducted in English (pp.43–44). The aim of this teaching approach, according to MEXT, is to respond to the growing demand for L2 communicative competence related to globalization. In December 2013, MEXT released an expanded version of the guidelines, entitled the "English Education Reform Plan Responding to the Rapid Globalization"

(2013, p.1). The plan calls for this "teaching English through English approach" that is used for high school education to be applied to junior high schools as well by 2020. Moreover, the plan suggests that the high school English classes should be conducted not "principally in English" but "in English." In other words, MEXT stipulates that it is desirable for the six years of English education in junior and senior high schools to be conducted in English regardless of students' goals for English study or the purpose of individual lessons.

These guidelines seem to be linked to the ideas of Communicative Language Teaching (CLT), which has been widely encouraged for English classroom teaching. CLT can be generally explained as an L2 teaching approach that emphasizes the importance of L2 communicative competence, which is applicable to authentic situations. Therefore, students are encouraged to learn the target language through its use instead of following the given instructions of the teacher (Brown, 2014, pp.235–236). Although there are some variations (e.g., weak and strong versions of CLT), the approach tends to eliminate students' L1 during the lesson. According to Ho and Wong (2004), CLT has become the dominant language teaching apporach in many Asian countries where English is learned as a foreign language (EFL). With the spread of CLT, however, various practical problems have been reported. Littlewood (2013) summarized those problems as follows: (a) Teachers tend to face difficulties in teaching and managing the class only through English; (b) Most students do not have adequate English proficiency to fully participate in an English-mediated CLT lesson; and (c) The CLT approach does not necessarily aim for students to prepare for a traditional memory-based examination (p.7). Considering the fact that CLT has been developed under English as a second language (ESL) education, Littlewood suggests that EFL classrooms should adjust the CLT approach to their own environment (p.360). Likewise in Japan, it may be necessary to have more cautious discussion and extended research in implementing the new teaching guidelines at junior and senior high schools.

Another example that reflects the current trend in Japan is the promotion of English-mediated instruction at the university level. It is reported that 262 out of 762, or roughly 36% of Japanese universities offered such classes at the undergraduate level in 2013 (MEXT, 2015). The Education Rebuilding Council (2013) recommended that this trend be further promoted in order to create an educational environment adapted to globalization (p.2). This seems a useful approach to attract foreign students who have a good command of English but limited Japanese language skills. The question, however, is how many average Japanese university students are capable of fully understanding English-mediated lectures on a serious academic topic. According to a survey conducted by MEXT (2015), nearly 70% of third-year high school students were categorized as A1 level for English reading and listening skills under the Common European Frame of Reference for Languages (CEFR), and over 80% of them were A1 level for English writing and speaking skills. The A1 level of CEFR is equivalent to the third-grade test of the Society for Testing English Proficiency (STEP), which is the target level for junior high school graduates. In light of the average English proficiency level of third-year university-track high school students, English-mediated classes at second-tier or lower universities may not represent the best approach for deepening an understanding of specialized subjects or encouraging lively classroom interaction. It seems necessary for them to have some kind of support in order to understand the content of academic lectures in English.

As discussed above, the current trend of English education in Japan seems to include some possible problems, which can be summarized as the following two points worth considering. One is the general assumption underlying the new teaching trends, and the other is the lack of consideration of students' perceptions and their learning environment. The first point concerns the assumption at the basis of the new teaching trend toward increasing L2 use in the classroom as a means of directly promoting L2 learning, regardless of the specific circumstance. With regard to L2 learning, in general, there seems to be no empirical research that demonstrates a direct relation between the increase of L2 use and the enhancement of L2 learning. If the goal of instruction is to promote L2 learning, the focus should be not only on the quantity of L2 use in the classroom but also on how the L2 is used to support students' learning processes. Even if the L2 is used throughout a lesson, for instance, there is a possibility that students' L2 output will be limited or remain at a superficial level as compared to their cognitive development. In order to facilitate the learning process, students need to bridge the gap between their L2 skills and their cognitive resources. Students' L1 can be a useful tool to promote L2 learning in terms of the various cognitive and affective advantages that L1 use brings (Butzkamm, 2003; G. Cook, 2010; V. Cook, 2008; Cummins, 2007),.

The second point of concern is the lack of consideration for students' perception of the "language use in either the L1 or L2" (henceforth referred to simply as "language use") and their learning environment. The latest survey conducted by MEXT (2014) regarding language use in the L2 classroom shows the percentage of L2 use by teachers and the portion of L2 language activities conducted by students. That is, nearly 10% of the teachers use the L2 "most of the time" (defined as "75% or more of the class time") and nearly 9% of the English classes allocate 75% or more of the class time to L2 language activities. The survey does not report, however, how students perceived their language use. Such cognitive and affective factors seem worthy of consideration since they could influence students' participation, motivation, and learning outcome. For instance, in the case of adult learners, who are cognitively mature yet incapable of fully expressing their thoughts in the L2, they tend to experience what Brooks-Lewis calls "classroom shock," i.e., feeling stress about a classroom environment where the teacher controls the language use for asking questions or for having students answer questions (2009, p.224). This mental stress may be escalated by enforced L2 use, which could possibly discourage students' classroom participation. Moreover, novice students who are unable to understand teachers' instruction via the L2 only are usually unable to ask a confirmation question in the L2 either. Under such conditions, it is difficult for students to maintain their motivation. If partial L1 use would ease the way for students to participate in the lesson as well as boost their motivation, there seems to be no reason to exclude it from the L2 classroom.

In addition, no adequate attention has been paid to students' learning environment. In the case of Japan, where students are learning English as a foreign language and the majority of teachers and students share a common first language (Japanese), targeted L1 use in the classroom can bring great advantages. Such advantages are not usually available in the case of an English as a second language environment. It is typical in an EFL environment for students to have few opportunities to use English outside the classroom. That is to say, learning English inductively is almost impossible due to the limited opportunities for L2 use outside the classroom. Taking these conditions into consideration, it may be more efficient for teachers to use the shared L1 to provide a certain amount of explicit instruction about the language or the content of a lesson to EFL students, thereby enabling them to learn the L2 more efficiently through a more or less deductive manner. At the same time, it is equally important for those EFL students to have ample opportunities to use English in a meaningful context in the classroom. Littlewood (2014) calls these requirements under the EFL environment as a twofold focus of L2 learning and teaching, consisting of "analytical activities" and "experiential activities." In other words, analytical activities can encourage students to learn about the language, while experiential activities can provide students with a meaningful context to use the language for learning. In order to facilitate L2 learning in the EFL environment, these activities can be combined effectively during the lesson. Moreover, it is necessary for students to understand the analytical activities, which provide them with linguistic knowledge and necessary information for the experiential activities. In accordance with students' English proficiency levels, therefore, partial L1 use during analytical activities can help promote students' participation in experiential activities.

To summarize, the current trend of English education in Japan seems to encompass two potential problems. First, there seems to be too much reliance on the assumption that the increase of L2 use will directly enhance L2 learning regardless of students' proficiency levels or lesson content. Second, the issue of students' perception of language use and their learning environment do not seem to have been adequately considered. In order to overcome these problems, it is important to do research to examine if partial L1 use can be effective, as discussed above. Taking into account second language acquisition (SLA) theories and empirical research, it seems possible to find out more appropriate ways to use the L1 as a support for L2 learning. Based on these arguments, the researcher conducted the current study in line with the purpose outlined below.

B. Purpose of the Study

1. Focus

The current study focuses on Japanese university students (novice and upper-intermediate levels) who are learning English as a foreign language (EFL). Although their learning environment is officially categorized as EFL, the researcher uses the term "L2" in order to make a contrast with "L1" (Japanese). Therefore, in the current study, L1 denotes Japanese and L2 represents English. Furthermore, the definition of L1 and L2 in the current study corresponds, respectively, to "own language" and "new language," as defined by G. Cook (2010, pp.xxi–xxii).

The intention of the current study is to examine the effects of partial L1 use for L2 learning. For this purpose, the current study focuses on reading skills. This choice was made because the cognitive process of reading has been studied extensively for many years. It is a great advantage for the researcher to be able to refer to the results of previous research. In addition, in a reading class it is relatively easy for the researcher to control the level, type, and amount of L2 input as well as the focus of students' L2 use. Moreover, most Japanese university students are accustomed to answering comprehension and summary questions based on a written text as a measurement of reading. These advantages enable the researcher to obtain reliable data for the purposes of the current study.

It is also important to clarify in the research who is using the L1 and how it is being used. In the current study, the L1 was used for peer interaction during pair work. That is, the participants were asked to discuss seven focus questions regarding a reading text prior to taking a summary completion test. One group had the pair work in their L1

(Japanese), and the other group did the same task in the L2 (English). The results of pair work were measured by the scores of focus questions and the elicited recordings of pair work. To examine the influence of pair-work language use on reading comprehension and reading attitudes, a summary completion test, a delayed summary completion test, and a post-research questionnaire were conducted.

The current study also focuses on peer interaction on the basis of the following three conditions. First, a post-reading peer interaction activity was conducted. Since the researcher had examined the effects of language use during pre-reading peer interaction activities on L2 reading in the previous research (Matsumoto, 2013), the current study aimed to examine the same variable with regard to post-reading activities. By combining these two studies, it became possible for the researcher to discuss the issue more or less holistically. Second, the current study focused on peer interaction in order to examine the influence of language use on L2 reading from the students' perspective. As explained previously, it is important to examine actual students' language use and their comprehension in discussing the research focus of the current study. Third, pedagogically speaking, having peer interaction is considered valuable in terms of L2 learning as well as reading comprehension. Therefore, it seemed worth having peer interaction even as a part of experiment.

To summarize, in order to reveal the influences of language use on L2 reading comprehension and reading attitudes, the current study focuses on peer interaction in the form of pair work as a post-reading activity. More specifically, the five variables that the current study examines are reading comprehension, results of pair work, evaluation of pair work, language preference for pair work, and language preference for different circumstances during a lesson. Consequently, the results will indicate some pedagogical hints on how to facilitate L2 learning and reading comprehension via the partial L1 support.

2. Goals

There are two primary goals of the current study. The first goal is to examine the effects of language use during peer interaction on L2 reading. The second goal is to theoretically and empirically present the ways to facilitate L2 learning via partial L1 support.

In order to achieve the first goal, it is necessary to conduct wide-ranging, long-term research across the four skills of English, while targeting various levels of students. Due to limited time and resources, however, the current study focuses on the reading classes at novice and upper-intermediate levels at Japanese universities as a starting point. This seems to be an appropriate place to begin the research for the reasons discussed in the previous section. In addition, university students are cognitively the most mature students within the educational system, and also they embody the results of the six years of English education in junior and senior high school. By examining university students, therefore, it seems possible to identify some pedagogical implications for other educational institutions as well. If the current study can indicate some effects of L1 and L2 peer interaction on L2 reading, it could help teachers to make sensible decisions regarding language use in the L2 classroom.

The other goal of the current study is to make pedagogical suggestions regarding how to promote L2 learning via partial L1 support. Although various advantages of L1 use during the L2 lesson have been illustrated by numerous researchers, the trend of English education in Japan influenced by MEXT now leans toward exclusive L2 use and the elimination of the L1. Given the situation above, it would be beneficial to identify practical ways to facilitate L2 learning via partial L1 support in accordance with levels of students and types of lessons. This paper, therefore, will investigate effective language use in the L2 reading classroom by referring to both SLA theories and empirical research, such as the influence of language use on L2 learning, on L2 reading, and on peer interaction.

The organization of this paper is as follows. The literature review in Chapter II presents the theoretical basis of the current study and clarifies the central research questions. Chapter III describes the current study in detail and presents its results. Chapter IV discusses the results, deduces pedagogical implications, mentions limitations, and offers suggestions for future research. Finally, Chapter V concludes the paper.

Chapter II
Literature Review

As presented in the previous section, the current study explores the influence of language use on L2 learning. In particular, the study examines the effects of L1 and L2 use during peer interaction in the form of pair work on L2 reading. This section reviews several SLA theories and studies in order to provide a theoretical basis for the current study. First, the theoretical background of L1 use in the L2 classroom is briefly summarized from two perspectives: one is an overview of principal language teaching methods and approaches, and the other is empirical research which is aimed at grasping the current situation of language use in the classroom. Second, the researcher will present some theoretical argument in support of L1 use in the L2 classroom by referring to Cummins' concept of "common underlying proficiency (Cummins, 2001)," "multi-competence" proposed by V. Cook (2008), and several sociolinguistic aspects related to the current role of English. Third, the pedagogical benefits of L1 use in the L2 classroom will be discussed from the perspective of students and of teachers. Fourth, in relation to the focus of current study, the researcher will describe the basic mechanism and features of L2 reading, with a focus on the following three points: (a) reading models, (b) unique features of L2 reading, and (c) circumstances of L1 and L2 use for L2 reading. Fifth, also in relation to the focus of the current study, the effects of peer interaction on L2 learning and reading will be examined. Based on these arguments as well as the previous research (Matsumoto, 2013) that examined the effects of L1 and L2 pre-reading activities on L2 reading, the researcher will propose hypotheses regarding the effects of L1 use on L2 reading and ultimately L2 learning. Finally, the researcher will present the research questions designed to examine the effects of L1 and L2 use during peer interaction in the form of pair work on L2 reading.

A. Language Use in the L2 Classroom

The current study intended to explore the effects of language use on L2 learning. In order to examine this rather broad theme, the researcher began by narrowing down the focus to language use during peer interaction in the L2 reading lessons. This section, therefore, will discuss the following three core segments of the study: (a) L1 use in the L2 classroom, (b) effects of language use in relation to L2 reading, and (c) effects of language use in relation to peer interaction.

1. Background of L1 use for language instruction and learning

Students' L1 use in the classroom has been treated differently according to teaching methods and approaches. In order to present how and when the L1 has been used in the L2 classroom, the researcher will first examine several teaching methods and approaches, with a focus on language use. Then the researcher will introduce the latest empirical research on L1 use in the English classroom to elucidate the current situation.

a. Methodological perspectives: To use or not to use

This section will provide a brief overview of how students' L1 has been regarded depending on different teaching methods and approaches.

The researcher chose six teaching methods and approaches that have a clear indication or unique way of language use. The following description of each method or approach is mainly based on Brown (2014) and Celce-Murcia (2014), while the historical background refers mainly to Howatt (2004). This section will use the term "target language (TL)" instead of "L2" because teaching methods in general are used not only for the L2 but also for the L3 or additional languages.

The Grammar Translation Method, which originated in Germany at the end of the 18th century, provides students with grammar instruction along with word-lists and translation exercises (Howatt, 2004, p.132). Since the goal of instruction under this method is to enable students to read a text in the TL, listening and speaking skills are not focused in the classroom. Therefore, the L1 is exclusively used for the teacher's instruction and students' production during the lesson.

The development of transportation system in Europe and elsewhere, beginning around the 1840s, led to a rapid increase in demand for face-to-face communication via the TL. This in turn led to growing criticism of the Grammar Translation Method by the end of the century, giving birth to new teaching methods, such as the Direct Method. The Direct Method aims to simulate the L1 acquisition process in the TL classroom. The correct use of expressions and pronunciation are emphasized under this method, and the L1 use is not allowed for either instruction or production.

Implementing the Direct Method in a school environment, however, was quite time- consuming and also costly, since it involved hiring skilled teachers and required small class sizes. The outbreak of World War II sparked an urgent demand in the United States and elsewhere for military personnel capable of acquiring oral proficiency in the TL within a short period of time. As a result, what came to be known as the "Army

Method" was created, which was later developed into the Audiolingual Method in the 1950s and 1960s. This method, which was influenced by the theories of behaviorism and structural linguistics, considers that language learning occurs through habit formation via pattern practice. In order to form good language habits, students are required to perform repeated drills using the TL.

Along with the development of studies on TL learner error analysis and their inter- language use, more attention started to be paid to TL learners' cognitive system and psychological aspects in the 1970s. As a result, new language teaching methods and approaches that took into consideration learners' affective factors were created. One example is Community Language Learning, where students can decide what to talk about instead of following the textbook or the teacher's instruction. That is, the teacher translates students' L1 utterances into the TL, which are recorded and practiced by students. The teacher also provides linguistic explanation via the L1 if necessary. As students' proficiency levels advance, the amount of teacher translation is reduced, but the TL is never enforced unless students voluntarily use it so that students' anxiety level can be kept low.

The period from the 1970s onward saw the development of studies on sociolinguistics, pragmatics, and discourse analysis. This led TL classrooms to focus more on language functions in a specific context as well as on TL learners' needs, which facilitated the development of Communicative Language Teaching. This approach focuses on enhancing students' communicative competence, which should be directly applicable to real-life situations. Although there are several variations under the approach (e.g., strong or weak version), the common point is to focus on practical TL use through meaningful or authentic interaction. For instance, by engaging in a task or a project, students are expected to learn the TL in context more or less inductively. In order to provide students with maximum exposure to the TL, the L1 is eliminated from the classroom.

In the 1980s, the Natural Approach was developed based on the five hypotheses presented by Krashen and Terell (1983): Acquisition-learning Hypothesis, Natural Order Hypothesis, Monitor Hypothesis, Input Hypothesis, and Affective Filter Hypothesis. Since addressing each hypothesis in details is beyond the scope of this paper, the researcher will focus on the basic points in relation to the language use. Under this approach, the teacher is expected to create a comfortable and non-threatening atmosphere in the classroom so that students will absorb the TL input that the teacher provides. The teacher uses the TL only, and students are encouraged to use the TL as well. In order to minimize students' anxiety, however, L1 use is allowed if necessary.

The summary of the language use in each method and approach is shown in Figure 1 below.

As Figure 1 shows, the majority of teaching methods and approaches encourage students and teachers to use the TL either primarily or exclusively.

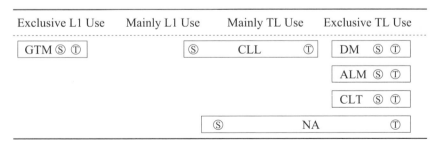

Figure 1. L1 and TL (L2) use in each teaching method and approach. Each abbreviation stands for: GTM (grammar translation method), CLL (Community Language Learning), DM (Direct Method), ALM (Audiolingual Method), CLT (Communicative Language Teaching), and NA (Natural Approach). S stands for "student" and T stands for "teacher."

V. Cook (2008) described this tendency as follows:

> With a few exceptions, the majority of teaching methods from the direct
> method to the audio-lingual method, to task-based learning, has insisted
> that the less the first language is used in the classroom, the better the
> teaching. (p.180)

The above quote points out the widely accepted assumption in the
field of language education: the less L1 is used in the classroom, the
more L2 learning will occur. The current study was conducted in order to
examine this widely held view. The following section will describe the
current situation of L1 use in the English classroom, referring to the latest
worldwide research.

b. Empirical research on L1 use in the English classroom

Hall and G. Cook (2013), based on questionnaires and interviews,
conducted research on how teachers and students around the world
use their L1 in the English classroom. In the research, 2,785 teachers
from 111 countries responded to the questionnaire, and 20 teachers
were interviewed among the participants. This research provides
useful information regarding the current situation of L1 use in the real
classroom. Among all the data, the researcher will focus on the following
three points in particular: (a) quantity and circumstances of L1 use, (b)
teachers' attitudes toward L1 use, and (c) the relation between students'
proficiency level and L1 use.

First, with regard to the quantity of L1 use, the research revealed
that 30.1 % of the teachers used the L1 "sometimes," 25.7% of them used
the L1 "often," and 16.2% of them used the L1 "always." The majority
of teachers used the L1 for the following four situations in particular:
explaining vocabulary (65%), explaining grammar (58.1%), building
rapport and good atmosphere (53.2%), and maintaining discipline

(50.4%). In addition, quite a number of teachers pointed out that the L1 is appropriate for metacognitive activities (e.g., discussing learning strategies, conducting needs analysis) as well as for comparing L1 and L2 grammar (p.15). As for students' L1 use, the teachers' observations revealed that the vast majority of students used their L1 during the lesson to some extent. The L1 was used most commonly by students for studying vocabulary and comparing L1 and L2 grammar (70%). Many students also used the L1 to confirm teachers' instructions in order to fully participate in language activities and to maintain good relations with their peers. Hall and G. Cook (2013) pointed out that students were using the L1 in order to create "a pedagogical and social environment in which language learning can take place" (p.16).

The second point concerns teachers' attitudes toward L1 use. The majority of the teachers surveyed strongly supported excluding (61.4%) or limiting (73.5%) L1 use. Yet, at the same time, many teachers were aware of the merits of L1 use. For instance, 56.7% of the teachers said that use of the L1 can help students express themselves during a lesson. The results supported Macaro's suggestion (2006) that "many teachers recognize the importance of English as the predominant, but not necessarily the only language in the classroom" (as cited in Hall and G. Cook, 2013, p.17). The teachers also indicated their reasons for either excluding or allowing L1 use. Their main reason against L1 use was that it deprives students of opportunities to hear and speak English. Other teachers pointed to the impracticality of using L1 in a multilingual environment or indicated that it would prevent students from thinking in English. In contrast, L1 use was supported above all for two reasons. Students can make use of pre-existing knowledge for L2 learning and students' anxiety in the L2 classroom can be reduced (p.18).

The third issue concerns students' proficiency levels. The majority of teachers agreed that L1 use is more suitable for lower-level students (p.19). At the same time, the majority of teachers strongly believed that higher-level students expect to have an English-only classroom (p.24). These results seem to indicate that many teachers are considerate of students' proficiency level in deciding language use for a lesson.

In conclusion, Hall and G. Cook (2013) emphasized the importance of finding out the optimal L1 use in the L2 classroom (p.26).

2. Theoretical support for L1 use

In order to develop the rationale behind L1 use for L2 learning, the researcher will present the following two concepts that indicate a connection between L1 and L2: "common underlying proficiency" (Cummins, 1984, 2001) and "multi-competence" (V. Cook, 1999). These two concepts have provided strong support for L1 use during the L2 lesson.

a. Common underlying proficiency

Based on his diverse bilingual education research, Cummins (1984) pointed out that the level of students' L1 linguistic and academic proficiency strongly influences L2 development (p.3). His concept of "common underlying proficiency" refers to "the cognitive and academic knowledge and abilities that underlie academic performance in both languages" (2001, p.173). This notion is illustrated as "the dual iceberg representation of bilingual proficiency" in Figure 2 on the following page.

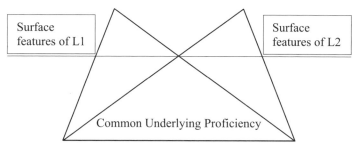

Figure 2. Dual iceberg representation of bilingual proficiency. Adapted from *Negotiating identities: Education for empowering in a diverse society (2nd ed.)* (p.174) by J. Cummins, 2001, Los Angeles: California Association for Bilingual Education. Copyright 2001 by California Association for Bilingual Education. Adapted with permission

The two tips of an iceberg on the surface of the water represent observable performance in two different languages, i.e., L1 and L2. Although those two tips seem independent from each other, they in fact share a great amount of cognitive resources, as indicated by the overlapped part underwater. Once students have reached the "language threshold" which is to say, once they have enough linguistic tools and the ability to use them at an adequate level, they will be able to utilize the shared cognitive resources for L2 performance. In fact, various research in the field of bilingual education has demonstrated the positive contribution of students' prior knowledge (i.e., common underlying proficiency) to academic development in L2 (Cummins, 2001, p.17). Considering the process of how one's prior knowledge has been generally accumulated, it is obvious that "the engagement of prior knowledge is inevitably mediated through L1" (Cummins, 2007, p.232). These arguments have clarified the inseparable connection between the L1 and L2 as well as the contribution of prior knowledge to L2 learning, which seems to be facilitated by means of L1 use.

The idea of common underlying proficiency sheds light on

advantages for L2 students. Adult students in particular have great resources for learning because of their fully developed cognitive systems, usually acquired via the L1, as well as access to ample knowledge and experiences through their memory. According to the research in the field of cognitive psychology, learning occurs by associating new objects to one's prior knowledge (Cromley, 2000). In other words, pre-existing knowledge works as a "filter and anchor" to process new information and store it in one's memory (Bransford, Brown & Cocking, 2000). This view seems to be applicable to the case of L2 learning as well. That is, by analyzing differences and similarities between the L1 and L2, students are able to understand L2 vocabulary and grammar rules effectively and to store them into their memory efficiently. Not only linguistic knowledge but also metacognitive knowledge, such as learning and reading strategies, can be elicited from the common underlying proficiency for L2 learning. These activities can be conducted most effectively via the L1, especially at the novice or intermediate level. In fact, many teachers recognize the advantage of L1 use for linking students' pre-existing knowledge to newly learned L2 objects (Hall & G. Cook, 2013). Once students realize that they already possess great resources, they are likely to be more motivated to learn.

b. Multi-competence

The second key concept is "multi-competence," defined by V. Cook as "the knowledge of more than one language in the same mind" (2008, p.231). L2 students, or what V. Cook called "L2 users," with multi-competence perceive L2 differently from the monolingual native speakers (2003, p.5). In other words, L2 learning is fundamentally different from L1 acquisition since another language already exists in the L2 student's mind. Moreover, L2 students in general are cognitively mature due to their previous experiences and pre-existing knowledge, unlike children who are learning their L1 (V. Cook, 2010a). When the fundamental differences between L2 students and monolingual native speakers are considered, it is rather strange for the majority of classrooms to set monolingual native speakers as the only valid model of L2 instruction. Based on these arguments, V. Cook (2013) has suggested that the goal of L2 learning should be to become a good L2 user, rather than a failure as a native speaker. Good L2 users can be defined as those who are capable of using the L2 for their own purposes and reasons, while preserving "their own identities as being from their own culture" (V. Cook, 2013, p.49). Moreover, L2 users stand on their own right, rather than being "an imitation of someone else" (V. Cook, 2003, p.4). If the goal of L2 learning is to foster good L2 users instead of becoming "like a native speaker" (NS), the majority of English teachers in Japan do not have to deny their own identity as non-native speakers (NNSs) of English any more. Instead, they can become their students' accessible role models as good L2 users. At the same time, students can see themselves as a user of two languages, with a unique linguistic and cultural background, instead of feeling like an inferior version of NSs.

The notion of multi-competence also suggests that people's L1 perception is influenced as a result of L2 learning. There are various studies to support this view (V. Cook, 2003, 2004, 2011). For instance, a study revealed that Japanese-English speakers (advanced level) perceived colors (blue and cyan) differently from monolingual Japanese speakers (Athanasopoulos, Sasaki, & V. Cook, 2004; as cited in V. Cook & Bassetti, 2011). Another study showed that English students whose L1 was Spanish, Greek, or Japanese tended to choose a sentence subject in their L1 differently from monolingual speakers of each language (V. Cook, Iarossi, Stellakis, & Tokumaru, 2003). These examples seem to indicate the mutual influence between the L2 (English) and L1. As these examples and other studies suggest, if the L1 and L2 are firmly connected to each other and perceptions formed by them are mutually influenced, it does not make sense to exclude students' L1 from L2 learning environment. As V. Cook (2004) criticized, it is "an illusion that permitting only the second language in the classroom forces the students to avoid their first language; it simply makes it invisible" (p.233).

To summarize, V. Cook's idea of multi-competence shows mutual connection between the L1 and L2, which also indicates fundamental differences between L2 students and monolingual native speakers.

c. Sociolinguistic perspectives: Changing roles of English

The two notions discussed above suggest a strong connection between the L1 and L2 that could provide sufficient theoretical support for L1 use in the L2 classroom. Bearing such theoretical grounds in mind, let us take a look at the environment surrounding English from a sociolinguistic perspective. Graddol (2006) has examined the current state of English from various perspectives, such as demographics, economics, sociology, technology, and politics. According to his study, 74% of the English communication in 2004 was trans-border communication between NNSs. This indicates that English interlocutors are more likely to be NNSs at present. Accordingly, more variations of English have been emerging and spreading across the world. Given this situation, the tradition of setting native speakers' English as the only norm does not seem suitable any more. It seems necessary to shift the goal of L2 teaching and learning toward the following three points: (a) intelligibility, (b) intercultural competence, and (c) knowledge of specialized fields.

First, intelligibility of oral communication can be defined as being able to recognize words and utterances; being able to understand the meaning of words and utterances in association with context; and being able to infer interlocutor's intentions (Smith & Nelson, 1985; as cited in

Pickering, 2006). The intelligibility of NNSs' utterances used to be judged by NSs according to the norms of NS English (Jenkins, 2000, p.69). However, with the increasing diversity of English use (e.g., English as a *lingua franca*, or World Englishes) as well as the increasing number of NNS interlocutors, intelligibility among NNSs has garnered more attention and various lines of research have been conducted to address this issue. For instance, Jenkins (2000, 2002) presented the notion of Lingua Franca Core, which illustrates essential features of pronunciation in order to increase intelligibility of NNS-NNS communication. Pickering (2006) also pointed out that interaction among NNSs is different from interaction among NSs or NS-NNS in terms of communication strategy use and accommodation processes. Hence, Pickering emphasizes the necessity of shifting the pedagogical goal from only targeting a NS model to a new model focusing on intelligibility among diverse NNSs (p.9). These arguments seem to suggest that teachers and students should be more aware of the importance of intelligibility, especially in the case of NNSs' communication, and learn about the strategies of communication and accommodation in order to enhance intelligibility (e.g., Jenkins, 2007; Seidlhofer, 2011). Such metalinguistic knowledge can be shared efficiently using the L1, and then students can practice using those strategies via L2 communicative activities, through a process of trial and error. People used to think that an EFL environment has the disadvantage of insufficient NS input or interaction with NSs. Considering the increasing importance of NNS communication, however, it could be argued that EFL has the advantage of offering a unique setting where most communication is conducted between NNSs, such as interaction between the NNS-teacher and students or among students. An EFL environment can be ideal for learning about NNS communication as long as the teacher can set up meaningful activities for L2 communication and help equip students with the necessary language tools and metalinguistic knowledge.

Second, it is necessary for students to enhance "intercultural competence" in the global setting of English communication. Byram, Nichols, and Stevens (2001) have defined intercultural competence as having knowledge about one's own culture as well as interlocutor's culture, associating one's culture to others', having a generous attitude toward other cultures, and evaluating each culture without any bias (pp.5–7). Interestingly, in all of these cases there is a dual perspective, focusing on both one's own culture and the culture of the interlocutor. That is to say, an adequate understanding of both cultures is indispensable to successful intercultural communication. In order for students to learn such information accurately and effectively, the L1 seems to be able to provide them with metacognitive support. In the real communication, *what* students know about intercultural competence is much more valuable than *how* they have learned it. Once students have come into possession of the necessary information for intercultural communication, they can develop their practical skills to overcome the linguistic difficulties and bridge cultural differences in various L2 activities (see also Language use and twofold focus of L2 learning and teaching in Chapter IV).

Finally, for the success of English interaction in a global setting, students need to have an adequate amount of content-related knowledge in a specialized field. Even if someone has a great command of English, few people will listen to that person unless he or she has some meaningful content to convey. People are more interested in the value of the offered information than the speaker's degree of fluency. Therefore, cultivating one's knowledge in a specialized field is as important as enhancing language proficiency. In this regard, depending on students' English proficiency, teachers can use the L1 to convey certain content knowledge, such as newly introduced concepts or complicated theories. The L1 also can be beneficial for students to develop their own ideas and share them with peers through having an active and in-depth discussion without any linguistic burden.

In short, there has been a drastic change in the status and role of English, which has become a common communication tool for people around the world. In such a global setting, English interlocutors are often NNSs with different language and cultural backgrounds. Therefore, it seems important for L2 students to allocate their limited time not only to practice "accurate" pronunciation and expressions according to the native-speaker norm, but also to develop the intelligibility and intercultural competence necessary for global English communication. In addition, developing specialized content knowledge is crucial as well as cultivating language skills in order to be considered as a valuable interlocutor.

Considering these changes and the needs of present-day society, it seems inadequate to follow the traditional L2 teaching approach, whose ultimate aim has been for students to become "native-like" speakers of English. In today's global society, it is imperative for students and teachers to reconsider the goals of L2 learning and to work toward finding a new approach for L2 instruction.

3. Pedagogical support for L1 use

Pedagogically speaking, there are various advantages of L1 use for L2 learning and teaching. The researcher will first discuss the advantages from students' perspective and then consider the teachers' perspective.

a. Advantages of L1 use by students

The advantages of students' L1 use for L2 learning are mainly related to cognitive and collaborative aspects, which often overlap with each other. In short, the L1 use seems to facilitate students' cognitive processes as well as to encourage students' collaboration in the course of L2 learning. These advantages can be summarized as the following five points: (a) regulating cognitive process, (b) enhancing vocabulary learning, (c) increasing quality of L2 output, (d) enabling higher-level text comprehension, and (e) promoting collaboration.

i. Regulating cognitive process

According to Lantolf & Thorne (2006), the L1 regulates the cognitive processes in general and L2 learning is mediated by the L1 as well (p.215). Therefore, the researcher will discuss the L1's role of cognitive regulation by referring to the notions of "mental translation" and "private speech."

Kern (1994) defined "mental translation" as processing target language (TL) expressions into the L1 during L2 reading (p.442). The advantages of this type of L1 use are summarized as follows: (a) to reduce the burden on one's working memory by converting the text input into more familiar L1 expressions, (b) to prevent readers from losing track of the text meaning, (c) to store what readers comprehend in long term memory, and (d) to analyze a certain L2 expression syntactically (pp.449–453). Kern also pointed out that readers with higher language proficiency tend to use such mental translation for checking their reading comprehension during reading (p.453). These suggested roles of mental translation seem to echo research results by Upton and Lee-Thompson (2001), who utilized "think aloud" data and retrospective interviews to examine how L2 readers (10 Chinese ESL students, 10 Japanese ESL students, and post-ESL students) use their L1 while reading in accordance with their proficiency levels (intermediate, advanced, and post-ESL levels). Their findings showed that the higher-level readers hardly ever used their L1 merely to decode a text (e.g., trying to figure out the meaning of words or sentence structures); rather, they used the L1 as an efficient means of general text comprehension. Meanwhile, the lower-level readers benefitted from L1 use for decoding the text and monitoring their reading (p.491). Therefore, Upton and Lee-Thompson concluded that readers' L1 use is beneficial for all levels in different ways. Such studies seem to indicate that L2 reading is facilitated by cognitive regulation via the L1.

The other example of L1 use for cognitive regulation is related to the notion of "private speech," a term used in the field of sociocultural theory to refer to how people use language for regulating their cognitive activities (Lantolf & Thorne, 2006, p.202), whether talking to others (interpersonal interaction) or to oneself (intrapersonal interaction). In the case of intrapersonal interaction, children's private speech is generally used for focusing on a task, figuring out the ways to accomplish the task, and evaluating the outcomes of the task (Frawley, 1997). These functions bear a surprising resemblance to the reasons that students use their L1 during collaborative L2 tasks, as reported by various studies (Antón & DiCamilla, 1998; Scott & De La Fuente, 2008). In other words, L2 students are regulating their cognitive process by talking to each other (peer interaction) via the L1. Therefore, Lantolf & Thorne (2006) emphasized the value of L1 for mediating L2 learning, given the fact that it is extremely difficult, even for highly advanced students, to have L2 private speech (p.215). In this regard, the argument that L1 use would prevent students from thinking in the L2 seems unfounded.

ii. Enhancing vocabulary learning

With regard to vocabulary learning, the benefits of L1 use have been indicated in several empirical studies. One example is the study by Tian and Macaro (2012), which examined L2 vocabulary instruction for

80 Chinese university students under two conditions. One was the code-switching condition (Chinese-English) and the other was the English-only condition. The results indicated that code-switching condition had an advantage over English-only instruction. In their analysis, Tian and Macaro described how an L2 lexical item is learned and stored in one's memory. According to their analysis, many concepts that L2 lexis represent have been experienced through the L1 and therefore those concepts are strongly linked to the L1 lexical network. Moreover, they pointed out that lower-level L2 students tend to access L2 lexical items via the L1 equivalents, rather than directly through the concept itself (p.372).

In order to explain the potential contribution of students' L1 more clearly, next, the researcher will introduce several studies related to L2 lexical development. According to the Revised Hierarchical Model (Kroll & Steward, 1994), there are three components of a lexical network: L1 lexicon, L2 lexicon, and the conceptual store. Schrauf, Pavlenko, and Dewaele (2003) conducted research on bilingual lexical development, and described that in the case of weak bilinguals, the link between L2 lexicon and the conceptual store tends to be tenuous. In other words, they have not fully developed the direct route from L2 lexicon to the conceptual store; instead, they translate L2 lexicon into the L1 equivalent, then access the conceptual store. For more advanced bilinguals, however, there is little need for translation from L2 to L1 lexicon (p.4). Their results seem to suggest that it is inevitable for novice students to rely on their L1 lexical resources to learn L2 vocabulary until they build up a firm connection between L2 and the conceptual store. Moreover, when students learn a new L2 word expressing a complicated concept that does not exist in their own conceptual store, the new concept needs to be explained from scratch. In such a case, L1 instruction may be useful for those students who have limited L2 vocabulary. Therefore, it makes

Chapter II   Literature Review   *29*

sense that bilingual instruction for L2 vocabulary surpassed monolingual instruction in the studies described above.

There is another study that indicates a strong influence of L1 lexical network on L2 vocabulary learning. Wolter (2006) claimed that L1 lexical and conceptual knowledge strongly influences the process of L2 vocabulary learning. As support for this argument, Wolter referred to a mistake made by a Japanese student of English, who used an English expression, "narrow room" instead of "small room." This mistake originated from the student's L1 collocation. Since the student knew all the words (*narrow, small, and room*), it was clear that the problem stemmed from collocation rather than L2 vocabulary size. For further analysis, Wolter grouped L2 lexicons into two categories: "conceptual connection" and "conceptual modification." The term conceptual connection refers to paradigmatically related words that have a "hierarchical connection to each other," such as superordinates, subordinates, and hyponyms (p.745). According to Wolter, these conceptual connections can be integrated relatively easily into the L2 lexical network through L1 lexical or conceptual knowledge because the student only needs to memorize a new L2 label matching the L1 counterpart. The difficulty, however, lies in conceptual modification, which means "appropriate combination of L2 lexical items" (i.e., collocation). Such syntagmatic connections require students to restructure their L1 lexical and conceptual knowledge itself. As the previous example shows, the Japanese student needs to realize the L1 collocation "narrow-room" is unique to the L1, and then to build up the new L2 collocation "small-room." In this regard, students' metalinguistic awareness needs to be raised.

These examples seem to provide significant indications regarding the sort of language use necessary for L2 vocabulary instruction. For instance, conceptual connections can be introduced based on the L1 lexical and conceptual knowledge using such L2 activities as lexical mapping, pairing quizzes on synonyms or antonyms, and categorizing superordinate or subordinate words. On the other hand, in the case of grasping conceptual modifications, students could benefit from having metalinguistic analysis on the differences between L1 and L2 collocations. Depending on the students' proficiency level, such analytical activities can be conducted in the L1, which will raise students' awareness and lead to vocabulary learning efficiently.

The studies described above seem to support L1 use for L2 vocabulary learning, particularly at the introductory stages of learning, where students' L2 vocabulary is too limited to understand the teacher's explanation via the L2. As discussed previously, students need to associate new information with pre-existing knowledge for their learning (Bransford, Brown and Cocking, 2000; Cromley, 2000). Likewise for L2 vocabulary learning, the pre-existing L1 lexical network can be used effectively to stabilize newly learned L2 words in the L2 lexical network.

iii. Increasing quality of L2 output

It is a common dilemma, especially for adult L2 students, that L2 linguistic proficiency is not quite high enough to fully express a complicated idea or to share deep knowledge about a given topic with their peers. As a result, some L2 students end up only expressing what they are able to say within their limited L2 language resource, regardless of their true opinions or interests. Butzkamm (2003) suggested that partially using the L1 in the L2 classroom could alleviate such frustration among students. According to him, having real L2 communication and banning L1 use constitutes a "conflicting demand" (p.33). If a lesson truly intends to include L2 communicative activities that are meaningful and interesting for students, the L1 needs to be efficiently used at the preparatory stage for their L2 production.

Indeed, there is a study examining the effect of bilingual and monolingual support on improving speaking proficiency (Macaro, Nakatani, Hayashi, and Khabbazbashi; 2012). The participants in the study were 49 Japanese university students enrolled in a three-week study-abroad program in the United Kingdom; the data were collected via speaking tests and questionnaires. The results of the study indicated that the group of students that received bilingual support, which allowed them to ask questions in the L1 and to code-switch during discussions, showed a higher gain in fluency and overall speaking scores than the group that only received monolingual (L2-only) support and were discouraged from using their L1. The study also claimed that the bilingual support promoted "more complex oral production" than what the students could have attempted in the L2 without the bilingual support (p.11). In light of these results, bilingual support seems to expand the possibility of students' L2 production and heighten the quality of their L2 output.

iv. Enabling higher-level text comprehension

Another aspect to consider is the effect of L1 use on students' comprehension. Butzkamm (2003) pointed out that appropriate L1 support can help students to undertake more difficult texts (p.34). He suggested that students could read bilingual texts or that the teacher could apply Dodson's Bilingual Method (called "sandwich-procedure") by providing L1 translation between the repeated L2 sentences from the text (p.32). By using such approaches in the classroom, students may be able to focus on the meaning of a text without having to undergo a word-by-word translation. If some teachers hesitate to code-switch frequently during a lesson, Lyster (2014) provided a good solution in his lecture on content-language integrated learning (CLIL). The idea is to read the same book, especially storybooks, in each of the two languages, successively.

For example, students could read one chapter in English for the first lesson, and then read the next chapter in Japanese for the following lesson, and so on until they finish reading the entire book. In this way, the flow of the story and inserted Japanese reading would help students to understand the overall content.

Such L1 support seems to be preferred by many L2 students when the content of L2 input or texts becomes more difficult. For instance, Carson and Kashihara (2011) conducted research to examine preferences among Japanese university students regarding L1 support in the L2 classroom depending on their proficiency levels. The results showed that 80% of beginning-level students preferred L1 support, unlike the advanced-level students, who did not desire L1 support except in the case of challenging content. When the content of L2 materials became more difficult, demand for L1 support grew regardless of proficiency levels. In other words, even for the advanced students, it seemed helpful to have some kind of L1 support for understanding difficult content.

Regarding the benefits of L1 use for enhancing students' com-prehension, there is another study conducted by Sweetnam Evans (2011), who examined participants' language preference, i.e., either L1 or L2, for reading recalls and responses. In the study, five different types of English texts were given to fourteen upper-intermediate level students whose L1 was Korean. After reading the texts, the participants were asked to choose either Korean or English to produce written recalls and responses. They showed a strong preference to use the L1 (Korean) for both tasks, which seemed to enhance the quality of their recalls and responses. For instance, in their written responses, the participants were able to explore their discussion at a high academic level (e.g., text genres and structures), which might not have been possible via the L2 (p.53). Sweetnam Evans analyzed the results as follows: The L1 use enabled L2 readers "to access their L1 reading skills and promote the construction of strong situation model and textbase characteristic of skilled L1 reading and essential to any comprehension, learning or long-term memory storage" (pp.49–50). In other words, by using the L1 in the cognitive process and production, the participants were able to attain higher level of comprehension as well as to fully express the outcome as a written form.

Considering these results, which point to the increase in demand for L1 support as the difficulty of the L2 tasks or texts increases, appropriate L1 support seems beneficial not only to enhance comprehension but also to open up opportunities for students to undertake more challenging L2 texts or tasks.

v. Promoting collaboration

L1 use seems to facilitate students' collaboration cognitively and affectively. As Carless (2008) described, the L1 use enables students to construct "scaffolded assistance" during peer interaction (p.331). The following empirical studies support this idea. Storch & Wigglesworth (2003) conducted a study to examine students' L1 use during joint reconstruction and composition tasks. They showed that students' L1 can be a useful tool with regard to enabling students to take control of their given tasks; letting them engage with the task "at a higher cognitive level"; and encouraging them to help each other, which enhances learning (p.768). Forcing students to use limited linguistic resources (i.e., exclusive L2 use) can result in relatively shallow discussions or missing valuable learning opportunities that could have been gained through peer scaffolding.

With regard to collaborative writing tasks, Antón and DiCamilla (1998) reported similar results. They examined five pairs of university students who were beginning-level Spanish students. The research found that the students' L1 (English) was an important "psychological tool" for completing tasks, and that the L1 was effectively used for providing peer scaffolding, maintaining and facilitating the collaboration for completing the tasks, and externalizing individual inner speech for coordinating cognitive activities. Considering all these benefits of L1 use, Antón and DiCamilla asserted that the students' L1 can be used as "powerful tools for learning" (p.245).

Lehti-Eklund (2013) observed a Swedish lesson in a Finnish upper secondary school. The research examined 17 students who had studied Swedish for five years. The students engaged in two types of communicative activities in pairs: discussing Swedish vocabulary and Q&A interaction in Swedish. During the pair work, the researcher observed how the students would code-switch in accordance with types of interaction. The findings revealed that the L1 (Finish) was used for maintaining interaction, while the target language (Swedish) was used to deal with information related to a given task. Lehti-Eklund found that the participants' L1 played a significant role to efficiently solve problems of interaction, enabling the participants to return to the main task quickly (p.148).

As these research results indicate, it seems rational to make use of the L1 for collaboration among students. According to Swain and Lapkin (2000), in order to facilitate L2 learning, it is crucial to have "collaborative dialogue" in which students solve problems and develop their knowledge in a collaborative manner (p.254). L1 use should be allowed as long as it facilitates such collaboration. Moreover, students' collaboration through peer interaction can bring positive results, such as increasing students' autonomy, participation, and motivation.

As the above-mentioned research results indicate, there are various advantages of students' L1 use in both cognitive and collaborative aspects. If used appropriately, students' L1 can contribute significantly to

L2 learning.

b. Advantages of L1 use by the teacher

This section discusses how teachers' L1 use can benefit L2 instruction. The advantages are mainly divided into three categories: efficiency, accuracy, and classroom management such as building rapport and maintaining discipline. The researcher will present research related to each category on the following page.

i. Efficiency

It is a well-known fact among teachers that time management is one of the most important yet difficult aspects of teaching. Often teachers have to cover a lot of content in a limited amount of time, thus requiring them to allocate time carefully during the lesson in order to focus on the essential activities, such as communicative activities using the L2 in a meaningful context. Using L1 in the classroom can be a useful way for teachers to manage their time more efficiently. Needless to say, the teacher should be encouraged to use the L2 for simple instructions, which are often called "classroom English," since students can understand them with the help of context and repetition. However, when "the cost of the target language is too great" in order to set up a rather complicated activity or to provide in-depth explanation about a concept, V. Cook (2001) has advised teachers to generally use the L1 (2001, p.418). The important point is to set up an appropriate learning environment so that all students can fully participate. Moreover, by making the instruction concise, the teacher can allocate ample time for L2 activities. Hence, the argument against L1 use, claiming that L1 use will reduce the amount of L2 use, does not stand up to close scrutiny.

ii. Accuracy

The issue of the accuracy of instruction overlaps to some extent with the topic of efficiency. In the case of grammar and vocabulary instruction, it can be rather difficult for the teacher to explain complicated grammar rules or abstract meanings of L2 words by using only the L2. Students at the novice or intermediate level in particular often struggle to understand grammatical terms. Moreover, V. Cook (2010b) noted that many teaching methods and approaches encourage teachers to convey the meaning of a target L2 word via the L2, which tends to require considerable time and effort. Here again, if the goal is to enhance students' accurate understanding of grammar rules or vocabulary, the L1 has a role to play.

Related to the accuracy of instruction, there are three more circumstances where the L1 can be useful. The first case is when the teacher checks students' comprehension. If students do not understand the instruction, the teacher needs to find out what has confused them. In an L2-only classroom, however, the teacher might overlook students' problems if their proficiency level is not high enough to use the L2 to pose a question or ask for help. In order to avoid this situation, the teacher can use the L1 to check whether students have understood the instructions accurately. The second occasion concerns error corrections. It seems beneficial to correct students' errors in the L1 in accordance with their needs; otherwise, lower-level students might sense only a negative tone of the teacher's correction without understanding the actual content of the correction. The third occasion is classroom announcements. When a teacher explains course requirements, assignments, or examinations, students are eager to understand the content of the information; they are not interested in checking their L2 listening comprehension.

iii. Building rapport and maintaining discipline

The other apparent advantage of teachers' L1 use is to provide students affective support in the classroom. L2 students in general tend to feel some degree of anxiety when learning a different language since they have a limited ability to understand input and generate output. As Brooks-

Lewis (2009) noted, this situation must be rather stressful, particularly for an adult L2 student "who is accustomed to having control over the direction of her or his actions." Therefore, it is important for the teacher to minimize students' "classroom shock" through support provided in the L1 (p. 224). In addition, having a good, trusting relationship with students is crucial for the teacher. Harmer (2001) suggested that the teacher should make use of the L1 to build rapport with students. When the teacher provides rather complicated feedback to students, whether it is positive, such as encouragement and advice, or negative, for instance correction and discipline, it should be conveyed accurately. Instead of taking a risk of L2 feedback in such circumstances, it seems better to make use of the L1 in line with student needs. By avoiding unnecessary miscommunication, the teacher can build up a solid foundation of trust with students.

In addition to building rapport, it is also important for teachers to consider classroom management and discipline. One common criticism of partial L1 use in the L2 classroom is that once L1 use is allowed, it spreads uncontrollably. Another concern is that students would get into the bad habit of relying on the L1 whenever they come across difficulties. This is precisely why the teacher needs to have solid classroom discipline regarding language use. Once the classroom rules are decided, it is important for the teacher to clearly explain the rules and the reasons behind them to the students. This seems to be one of the primary conditions in order to conduct an L2 lesson with principled L1 support. Depending on the students' proficiency level, it can be more effective to explain these rules in the L1.

One successful example of applying classroom rules for promoting L2 communication was provided by Liebscher and Dailey-O'Cain (2005). They conducted research on an advanced German class for English native speakers at the university level. On the first day of the German class, the teacher provided L1 explanation about language use, i.e., when and why to use the L1 or L2 at a given moment in a lesson. As a result, students were well-aware of the classroom rules, which in turn facilitated their L2 communication in the class.

All these studies discussed above indicate the advantages of teachers' L1 use in the L2 classroom, from both a pedagogical and an affective perspective. Some teachers, however, might still wonder exactly how much L1 use is appropriate or might want to determine the exact amount. As a general assumption, Macaro (2005) stated that as long as the teacher's L1 use is limited to 10% or less of the classroom discourse, there is no significant increase in students' L1 use. In order to make a sensible judgment about optimal language use, Harmer (2001) suggested considering the following four factors: (a) students' previous learning experience, (b) students' proficiency level, (c) the purpose of the course, and (d) the focus of the lesson (p.132). In addition, some sociolinguistic factors need to be considered, such as learning environment (ESL or EFL), classroom environment (monolingual or multilingual), and students' cultural background. After examining all these factors, each teacher should make a sensible decision about appropriate and effective language use.

B. Effects of Language Use on L2 Reading

In relation to the focus of the current study, which is to examine the effects of language use during peer interaction on L2 reading, the researcher will examine the following three aspects of L2 reading: (a) mechanism of reading, (b) unique features of L2 reading, and (c) circumstances of L1 and L2 use for L2 reading. The first aspect (mechanism of reading) needs to be examined more closely in order to reveal exactly how the language use would influence reading comprehension and reading attitudes in the process of reading. The second aspect (unique features of L2 reading) needs to be explored so as to identify efficient approaches to language use with regard to L2 readers. The third aspect (circumstances of L1 and L2 use for L2 reading) will help identify when and how to use the L1 and L2 in order to enhance L2 reading comprehension.

1. Mechanism of reading: Two reading models

Reading, in general, involves a very complicated process, wherein readers not only have to access their linguistic knowledge but also require background knowledge regarding the given topic. In the case of L2 reading, the situation can be even more complicated due to the fact that "L2 reading is an ability that combines L2 and L1 reading resources into a dual-language processing system" (Grabe, 2009, p.129). An enormous body of research exists on the topic of reading, with investigations on how people read and comprehend a text. Among such research, the researcher will introduce the following two examples: (a) schema theory, which has had a significant influence on the field of reading education; and (b) the construction-integration model (the CI model), which is a dynamic reading model to elucidate the process of reading.

First, in order to provide some background on schema theory, the researcher will refer to the well-known definition of reading as a "psycholinguistic guessing game" (Goodman, 1967). This view indicates that readers play the active role of constructing the meaning of a given text through "sampling from the input text, predicting, testing and confirming or revising those predictions, and sampling further" (Carrell & Eisterhold, 1983, p.554). In other words, instead of merely receiving text information as it is written, readers are creating meaning by associating the text information with their background knowledge, called "schemata." Readers' schemata function as a frame of reference, with a hierarchical structure ranging from the most specific to the most general (Carrell & Eisterhold, 1983, p.556). When reading a text, readers generally apply both top-down and bottom-up processing simultaneously. Top-down or conceptually-driven processing starts from the higher level schemata to make general predictions that can guide readers as they search for specific information in the text that corresponds to their predictions, while bottom-up or data-driven processing starts from text-based information that can activate the most specific, i.e., lower level schemata. Related schemata are then activated as the process moves on to the higher-level schemata. The constant interaction between top-down and bottom-up processing is thought to facilitate reading comprehension.

Schema theory has provided significant insights into reading comprehension, as well as useful pedagogical implications for reading instruction. For instance, studies based on schema theory have revealed the influence of culturally related background knowledge on reading comprehension, the importance of previewing related background knowledge for better reading comprehension, and the causes of failure to comprehend a text in relation to readers' misuse of (or lack of) schemata (Carrell and Eisterhold, 1983).

The second reading model that the researcher will present is the CI model (Kintsch, 1988, 1998). In contrast to schema theory, which grasps the role of background knowledge rather statically, the CI model describes a dynamic process of reading comprehension (Nassaji, 2002). In its original model (van Dijk & Kintsch, 1983), the process of reading comprehension was explained by the following three information processing stages: (a) surface representation (readers create certain

Chapter II Literature Review *41*

representation of text-based information by decoding the words and phrases of a given text), (b) textbase (readers construct a local network of propositions based on surface representation by checking coherence), and (c) situation models (readers associate textbase with their background knowledge and construct a coherent interpretation of the text).

In the revised model (Kintsch, 1988), the role of textbase was expanded to include not only propositions elicited directly from the text but also many other propositions "closely connected to it in the general knowledge net" stored in readers' mind like "a whole cluster" (p.180). Although this process might appear unnecessary or even wasteful, Kintsch explained that the cost of activating "irrelevant" material pays off because those seemingly irrelevant pieces of activated knowledge can provide readers with extra-cognitive resources to use in responding to unexpected inconsistencies of the text and adjusting to a new idea or concept to maintain "coherent" understanding. This seems to be a special point of the CI model; in other words, capturing flexible use of readers' background knowledge during reading.

The first two phases of reading, namely, processing surface representations and textbase, are also called the "construction phase," in which "nodes" are created in order to connect individual propositions obtained from the text (Rawson & Kintsch, 2004). The connection between nodes becomes stronger when they have more overlapping elements. Depending on the strength of the connection, some nodes are activated and passed on to the next stage of processing, while others remain inactivated and fade away; this is called the "integration phase." The cycle is repeated when readers move from a sentence to the next, thereby maintaining coherence between the sentences. At the same time, only the essential information is passed on to the next processing cycle.

As both schema theory and the CI model indicate, reading

comprehension is a result of interaction between text information and readers' background knowledge. Therefore, it is necessary for readers not only to activate linguistic knowledge but also to access appropriate background knowledge for text comprehension.

2. Distinctive features of L2 reading

This section focuses on the distinctive features of L2 reading. Compared to L1 reading, L2 reading is rather complicated since it requires readers both reading and L2 language skills. In attempting to shed light on the unique features of L2 reading, the researcher will discuss the following three notions: (a) the language threshold hypothesis, (b) the capacity theory of comprehension, and (c) the influence of limited L2 vocabulary on information processing.

First, one distinctive aspect of L2 readers is that even though they may have developed quite high L1 reading skills, their limited L2 language skills tend to hinder L1 reading skills from being transferred to L2 reading. This phenomenon can be explained by the theory of language threshold, which asserts that L1 reading skills are transferred only after L2 readers have reached a certain level of L2 proficiency (Clarke, 1980). When L2 readers exceed the threshold, Grabe (2009) noted that some of the reading skills and strategies would be more easily transferred, such as "phonological-awareness skills, word decoding, reading strategies, metacognitive awareness, [and] pragmatic skills" (p.144). Hence, pedagogically speaking, it seems effective for teachers to support students' text decoding phase by facilitating their lexical, syntactical, or structural analysis of the L2 text up to a certain level. Such analytical activities can be efficiently conducted in the L1, especially at the introductory stage. At the same time, it is important to raise students' awareness of their L1 reading skills, which is a valuable cognitive tool for L2 reading. For

Chapter II   Literature Review   *43*

instance, the teacher can ask students what kind of reading strategies they use for L1 reading and have them discuss what strategies are applicable to L2 reading. This type of metacognitive activity seems beneficial to boost students' confidence since they can become aware of their own cognitive resources. If necessary, this activity can also be conducted in the L1 as a warm-up activity prior to reading.

The second distinctive feature of L2 reading is illustrated by the capacity theory of comprehension (Just & Carpenter, 1992). This theory stated that when readers encounter a challenging reading task, they tend to allocate their limited cognitive resources more to lower-level processing, e.g., decoding text-based information, than to higher-level processing, e.g., making inferences or judgments about propositions elicited from the text. As a result, they tend to have difficulty in constructing an appropriate situation model, which requires readers to conduct both lower- and higher-level processing. Through her research, Horiba (1996) revealed that compared to L1 readers, L2 readers tend to focus more on lower-level processing and to pay little attention to the text structure, which results in a failure to create adequate situation models. One way to overcome this problem is to raise students' metacognitive awareness toward higher-level processing. For instance, the teacher could prepare focus questions or activities that encourage students to make inferences or judgments about the main ideas of a text. If necessary, students should be allowed to use the L1 for conducting such higher-level processing, e.g., predicting, inferencing, and judging, without being restricted by their limited L2 skills. One of the final goals of L2 reading instruction is to lead students to the stage where they can become independent readers capable of flexibly accessing higher- and lower-level text processing. As a bridge to this final goal, students' L1 could be used to guide them in a step-by-step manner.

Third, readers' L2 vocabulary is quite limited compared to their L1 vocabulary, which obviously causes problems for L2 readers, not only in decoding the text but also in processing text information. For efficient information processing during reading, text information should be kept compact by means of "integration, deletion, and generalization" so that readers can retain necessary information without overtaxing their cognitive resources (Ushiro, 2009, p.139). Toward that end, readers need to replace subordinate words or concepts with superordinate ones. But that is quite difficult to do since students tend to memorize each L2 lexical item separately without paying much attention to the connection between them. In order to raise students' awareness toward such lexical relationships among the L2 vocabulary, the teacher could make use of students' fully developed L1 lexical network. For instance, the teacher could ask students to associate various L1 words by using synonyms and antonyms or the combination of subordinate and superordinate words. Such activities will provide students with opportunities to realize how lexicons are connected to each other, which would also help them to develop their L2 lexical network. Since there is no one-to-one correspondence between the L1 and L2 lexical items, it seems important to do such awareness raising activities within either the L1 or L2 lexical network.

As discussed above, there are some distinctive features of L2 reading. In order to figure out efficient approaches for L2 reading instruction, teachers need to understand those features. In this regard, it seems beneficial to make use of students' cognitive resources, such as L1 reading skills and strategies or L1 lexical network for the sake of L2 reading instruction.

3. Circumstances of L1 and L2 use for L2 reading

In relation to language use and reading, it is important to consider when to use the L1 or L2 for enhancing reading comprehension. This section focuses on three studies to examine this point and suggest appropriate circumstances of L1 and L2 use during the reading lesson.

a. Levels of reading: Quality of textbase and degree of background knowledge use

As discussed above in the Mechanism of Reading section, reading comprehension can be defined as a result of meaning-construction for which readers integrate text information (textbase) and background knowledge. In other words, readers create mental representations of a text through the reading process. Coté, Goldman, and Saul (1998) explained that the quality of mental representation can be determined by two variables: "the quality of the textbase representation and the use of prior knowledge" (p.2). Their idea is summarized in Figure 3 below.

As Figure 3 shows, each quadrant represents a different level of mental representation (i.e., reading comprehension). First, fragmentary comprehension (lower left) means that readers can only understand pieces of information inconsistently, most likely due to a lack of

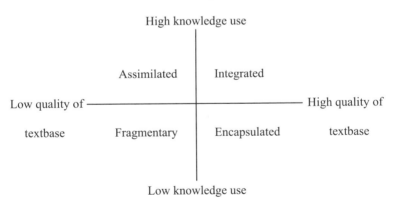

Figure 3. Four levels of mental representations of a text in line with the quality of textbase and the degree of prior knowledge use. Adopted from "Students making sense of informational text: Relations between processing and representation," by N. Coté, S. R. Goldman, & E. U. Saul, 1998, *Discourse Processes, 25,* p.3. Copyright 1998 by Taylor & Francis Group. Adapted with permission.

linguistic knowledge. In addition, readers do not (or cannot) associate their pre-existing knowledge with the text information. As a result, they fail to construct an appropriate situation model. Second, assimilated comprehension (upper left) might result in either a positive or negative result. Although the quality of textbase is still low, readers attempt to make use of their background knowledge. If they can elicit appropriate background knowledge, they are able to attain a better understanding of the text. Conversely, if readers refer to inappropriate background knowledge, they are not be able to understand the text sufficiently. This seems typical for the novice readers who tend to rely too much on their background knowledge without having adequate linguistic knowledge for text decoding. Third, encapsulated comprehension (lower right) is the stage where readers can create a rather high-quality textbase, but the information obtained from the text is not fully integrated into their existing knowledge. Although the quality of textbase may seem adequate, the degree of comprehension remains at a superficial level. Consequently, as Coté et al. pointed out, readers are not able to recall what they have read after a while due to little connection to the prior knowledge (p.4). Kintsch (2009) also described this type of reading as "understanding at the textbase level" without a construction of a solid situation model. The content cannot be stored as one's knowledge and can be easily forgotten (p.228). Finally, integrated comprehension (upper right) implies that readers can create an appropriate textbase and integrate it into their prior knowledge. In other words, readers can "digest" the text information and store it as a part of their cognitive network. At this stage, "real learning" seems to occur (Coté et al., p.3).

As the quadrants show, the outcomes of reading comprehension vary depending on the following two factors in particular: the quality of the textbase and the degree of background knowledge use. In order to aim for the highest level of reading comprehension, that is, integrated comprehension, teachers need to consider what kind of support and language use are effective at each stage. For instance, if students show only fragmentary comprehension, they need to have both linguistic and content-related support. At the level of assimilated comprehension, students need to construct a firm textbase, with linguistic support at the stage of decoding the text. In the case of encapsulated comprehension, students should be encouraged to integrate the text information obtained into their prior knowledge. In other words, more content-focused support would be effective.

In short, there are different levels of reading comprehension, and each level requires different types of support. In this regard, partial L1 use appears to be beneficial for certain situations. For instance, at the level of encapsulated comprehension, i.e., high quality textbase but little association with the prior knowledge, students should engage in in-depth content-related discussion via their L1 with no linguistic burden of L2 production. As a result, they could integrate the text information into their cognitive system. When exclusive L2 use is enforced, students' production is mostly limited to what they can say, and their discussions tend to remain at a superficial level. If the instruction intends to trigger content learning firmly anchored to students' cognitive system, the L1 should be used flexibly in accordance with their reading comprehension levels.

b. Settings of reading: Contextual clue and cognitive load

In order to discuss different settings of reading, the researcher refers to commonly known Cummins' quadrants, which include two continuums to categorize communicative activities: context-embedded versus context-reduced, and cognitively undemanding versus cognitively demanding (2001, pp.66–68). Although the quadrants originally focused on communicative activities, the categorization seems applicable to reading tasks because the two factors, that is, the amount of contextual clues and cognitive load, would greatly influence the outcome of the reading task as well. Figure 4 illustrates the notion of Cummins' quadrants below.

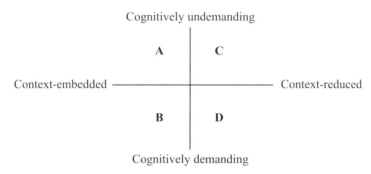

Figure 4. Four settings of a task with consideration to the range of contextual support and the degree of cognitive involvement. Adopted from *Negotiating identities: Education for empowering in a diverse society (2nd ed.)* (p.67) by J. Cummins, 2001, Los Angeles: California Association for Bilingual Education. Copyright 2001 by California Association for Bilingual Education. Adapted with permission

In Figure 4, the left parts of the horizontal continuum (quadrants A & B) represent tasks with ample contextual clues that would support students' comprehension and production, while the right parts (quadrants C & D) indicate tasks that require students to mainly rely on linguistic clues with few contextual clues. The upper part of the vertical continuum (quadrants A & C) shows tasks that require minimum cognitive load since the language tools necessary for the task are largely automatized. In contrast, the lower part of the vertical continuum (quadrants B & D) represents the tasks where students have to engage in a cognitively heavy load due to the fact that the necessary language tools are not fully automatized.

When it comes to L2 reading, quadrant A (contextual clue [+];

cognitive load [-]) is akin to a reading situation where students have a high level of language and cognitive ability to construct an appropriate textbase. In such a situation, there seems little necessity for students to use the L1 for linguistic or content support. Quadrant B (contextual clue [+]; cognitive load [+]) shows a case where students read a text with full of contextual clues but cannot create appropriate textbase due to lack of linguistic knowledge. Therefore, the linguistic support via the L1 seems effective to assist students' comprehension. The mirror image of quadrant B is quadrant C (contextual clue [-]; cognitive load [-]), where students' language ability is high enough, but few contextual clues are available. In such a situation, it would be useful for students to have L1 content support for better reading comprehension. Finally, quadrant D (contextual clue [-]; cognitive load [+]) indicates one of the most challenging reading situations, where students face a reading text with few contextual clues, having to rely on their limited language ability. This sort of situation is often found, for instance, in reading classes at the university level. Many Japanese universities require students to read academic texts in English, but those students who have little background knowledge on the subject matter and limited language ability would fail to learn either content or language. In order to avoid such a waste of time and effort, the L1 can be used for content and linguistic support in accordance with students' proficiency level.

To summarize, a setting of reading varies depending on its amount of contextual clues and degree of cognitive load. Therefore, it is necessary for the teacher to identify the setting of each reading task and devise the appropriate support in either the L1 or L2.

c. Influential factors for L2 reading: L2 language ability and L1 reading ability

Many researchers have explored the fundamental question: whether L2 reading is influenced by L1 reading ability or L2 language proficiency. In attempting to answer this question, Alderson (1984) noted that lower level readers tend to be more influenced by their L2 language ability, whereas higher level readers are more likely to be influenced by their L1 reading ability. This implies that L2 readers need to attain a certain L2 language proficiency, i.e., the threshold level, in order to make use of their reading ability acquired via the L1. According to Yamashita (2001), the influence exerted by each of the two factors of L2 reading comprehension changes according to readers' proficiency levels, which can be categorized as the fundamental, minimum, and maximum levels (pp.196–197). At the fundamental level, L2 reading comprehension is mainly influenced by readers' L2 language ability, and there is little influence from their L1 reading ability. At the minimum level, where readers are about to reach or go over the threshold level to comprehend a L2 text adequately, L1 reading ability starts to influence L2 reading comprehension, while the influence of L2 language ability gradually diminishes. At the maximum level, where readers have enough L2 language ability to decode the text appropriately, mainly the L1 reading ability influences the outcome of L2 reading. The relation between the three variables, i.e., L2 reading comprehension, L1 reading ability, and L2 language ability, is summarized in Figure 5 on the following page.

With regard to language use, the amount of L1 use seems to correlate to L2 language ability. Upton and Lee-Thompson (2001) pointed out that students' L1 reliance during L2 reading would decrease as their L2 proficiency increases (p.471). In relation to Figure 5, it may be beneficial for the fundamental-level students to have L1 support focusing on

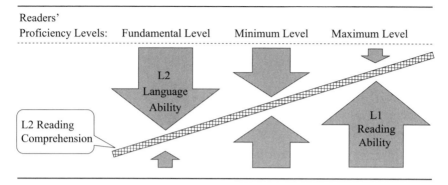

Figure 5. Influential factors of L2 reading comprehension.

the linguistic aspect of the text since their comprehension is primarily influenced by the L2 language proficiency. Along with the advancement of language proficiency, however, the amount of L1 support for linguistic aspects could be reduced. Instead, teachers can allocate more time on content-related discussion or awareness raising activities for metacognitive aspects, e.g., reading strategies, so that students can reach the integrated level of reading comprehension as Coté et al. (1998) suggested.

To summarize, it is crucial for the teacher to consider which factor — either students' L2 language ability or L1 reading ability — is more influential for individual teaching conditions and to decide on the appropriate support and language use. In this regard, Yamashita (2001) also pointed out that the degree of each influential factor could be fluid depending on the conditions of a reading task (p.197). Therefore, the above-mentioned levels of reading and settings of reading should be considered as well in order to provide effective L2 reading instruction.

Since reading is one of the most complex skills being studied in the fields of SLA research, it is beyond the scope of the current study to cover everything. The researcher, therefore, has discussed the following three points in relation to the focus of current study: (a) mechanism of reading, (b) distinctive features of L2 reading, and (c) circumstances of L1 and L2 use for L2 reading. These discussions seem to provide a solid basis for the current study.

C. Effects of Language Use on Peer Interaction

The current study focused on language use during peer interaction in the form of pair work after L2 text reading. Therefore, the researcher will briefly summarize how peer interaction influences L2 learning in general and how it is related to reading comprehension.

1. Effects of peer interaction on L2 learning

Generally speaking, peer interaction is considered to be beneficial in terms of enhancing the following four aspects: (a) quantity of students' output, (b) students' autonomy, (c) range of language function, and (d) corrective feedback (Yen-Chi, 2009). Ellis and Shintani (2014) have defined interaction as a "source of input and opportunities for output, which foster the internal processing that results in acquisition" (p.194), and they posed the fundamental question of how language learning arises out of interaction (p.202). In order to discuss this question, they refer to two theoretical frameworks: cognitive-interactionist theory and sociocultural theory. The researcher will examine these frameworks to consider how peer interaction contributes to L2 learning in general.

The first theoretical framework, cognitive-interactionist theory, can be represented by the following two well-known hypotheses: the interaction hypothesis (Long, 1983, 1996) and the comprehensive output hypothesis (Swain, 1985). According to the interaction hypothesis, language learning occurs through negotiation of meaning, where students try to make input mutually comprehensible via interaction. In addition, students can realize what they want to convey during interaction and then pay selective attention to a specific form which is suitable for the context. Consequently, input recognized through interaction is stored in individual interlanguage system (Long, 1983, 1996). The comprehensive output hypothesis, on the other hand, emphasizes the importance of output. By producing output, students' grammatical competence will be enhanced since they can (a) be aware of a problem, (b) test their hypothesis about the target forms and expressions, (c) review their L2 use consciously, and (d) eventually increase their control over L2 use (Swain, 1985). Although there are some differences between the two hypotheses, the key ideas can be summarized as follows. Interaction provides students with necessary opportunities and input for L2 learning, which is then processed and internalized within an individual student's cognitive system.

In contrast, sociocultural theory considers "interaction not as a source of data but as a site where learning occurs" (Ellis & Shintani, 2014, p.202). Originally, Vygotsky (1978/1997) introduced the idea of the zone of proximal development (ZDP) in which students can achieve a slightly higher level performance than their actual level with a help of more capable others. Expanding this idea, Swain and Lapkin (1998) reported that even similar level peers can be both experts and novices interchangeably. Ohta (1995) described the fluid relation between the novice and expert, which she called a "collaborative scaffold" whereby both students can contribute to learning (p.97). For instance, students can help each other by asking questions, negotiating solutions, sharing opinions, and facilitating communication via interaction. As Swain, Brooks, and Tocalli-Beller reported (2002), such mutual learning via peer interaction is observed in various activities of listening, speaking, reading, and writing (pp.173–181). In addition, sociocultural theory considers that language mediates one's own thinking and learning, whether used for talking to oneself (private speech: Lantolf, 2000) or talking to others (social talk: Swain, 2006). This also illustrates how crucial both intrapersonal and interpersonal interactions are to language learning.

Although peer interaction for L2 learning is defined differently, both cognitive-interactionist theory and sociocultural theory approve the crucial role of interaction for language learning.

2. Effects of peer interaction on L2 reading

This section examines the relations between peer interaction and L2 reading in particular by introducing the following two studies. First, Klinger and Vaughn's research (2000) revealed the positive influence of collaborative strategic reading during ESL content classes. The participants were 37 English-Spanish bilingual elementary school students who were given collaborative reading tasks (peer interaction) while reading the content class text. In order to enhance their reading comprehension, the following four instructed reading strategies were employed, which were previewing (sharing background knowledge), identifying difficult words or concepts in the text and using fix-up strategies, rephrasing the main ideas of each segment, and summarizing the text and predicting focus questions that the teacher might ask. During the peer interaction, the participants were able to help each other to co-construct the text meaning, and they showed a significant gain on the vocabulary test. In conclusion, Klinger and Vaughn emphasized the importance of teaching reading strategies regarding how and when to help each other during peer interaction in order to facilitate reading comprehension.

The second study regarding peer interaction and reading comprehension was conducted by Van den Branden (2000). The study examined 151 primary school children aged 10 to 12 at eight different schools, and compared the following four reading conditions: (a) unmodified written input, (b) pre-modified written input, (c) unmodified written input + oral negotiation with a peer, and (d) unmodified written input + oral negotiation with the rest of the class. According to the results, the groups that undertook oral negotiation, i.e., conditions (c) and (d), outperformed the other groups in terms of reading comprehension. Moreover, in this study, oral negotiation in the classroom was more beneficial than the negotiation between peers. It can be assumed that the class discussion led by the teacher might have had a clearer focus in order to enhance reading comprehension. Van den Branden suggested that "negotiation of meaning has particularly promising effect on the comprehension of written input if the students themselves are actively involved in signaling their problems and in trying to solve them" (p.438).

As discussed above, peer interaction plays a significant role in promoting L2 learning. Peer interaction provides students with an opportunity to negotiate meaning, identify problems, test hypotheses, and practice language use. According to sociocultural theory, interaction could be either interpersonal (peer interaction) or intrapersonal (private speech), both of which regulate cognitive process and mediate learning. Bearing this in mind, the researcher will suggest some appropriate circumstances of L1 and L2 use for peer interaction. For instance, when students are focusing on an analytical aspect of language, such as comparing L1 and L2 grammar rules and lexicons or having preparatory activities for L2 communication, it seems more efficient to use the L1 — except for the case of highly advanced students. On the other hand, if the focus is to practice L2 use through communication, students should be encouraged to use the L2 throughout the activities. It might be useful for students to have a review session in the L1 after such L2 activities so they can analyze their performance in order to aim for subsequent improvements.

In relation to L2 reading, it also seems beneficial to have peer interaction. According to the research studies, instruction on collaborative strategic reading encouraged students' helping behavior and supported their reading comprehension and language learning. Moreover, having collaborative discussion on written texts enhanced students' comprehension compared to those who did not undertake such discussion. If students' reading comprehension is enhanced, collaboration or discussion itself can be conducted with the support of partial L1 use until students reach a certain proficiency level. Such findings seem to support the idea of the current study, which focused on language use during peer interaction for L2 reading comprehension.

D. Hypotheses on the Effects of Language Use during Peer Interaction on L2 Reading

The above literature review has led the researcher to form some hypotheses regarding the theme of the current study. The hypotheses have also relied on the previous research (Matsumoto, 2013). In this section, therefore, the researcher will briefly summarize the literature review as well as the previous research, then will present hypotheses on the effects of language use during peer interaction for L2 reading.

1. Summary of the literature review
The following three points can be indicated.
■ L1 use is beneficial to L2 learning by supporting students' cognitive process and collaboration, increasing efficiency and accuracy of

teachers' instruction from the students' point of view, and enhancing such classroom management factors as building rapport and maintaining discipline through the teacher's L1 use.

■ L1 use is beneficial to L2 reading comprehension and memory retention by activating and sharing background knowledge, reducing readers' cognitive load, and facilitating deeper cognitive processing.

■ L1 use is beneficial for peer interaction not only by facilitating information exchange but also by enhancing collaboration with no pressure associated with L2 production, both of which seem to contribute to enhancing reading comprehension.

2. Summary of previous research (Matsumoto, 2013)

The previous research focused on pre-reading activities (PRAs), with the intention of clarifying the influence of language use on L2 reading comprehension and reading attitudes of the intermediate-level Japanese university students. The detailed description of the study will be found in Appendix A. The main findings of previous research can be summarized briefly in the following four points.

■ Different language use during pre-reading activities (PRAs) did not have a significant impact on reading comprehension (i.e., the results of reading comprehension tests and summary writing tasks) for either the familiar or the unfamiliar topic.

■ The participants' evaluation of PRAs in relation to reading comprehension tests did not indicate any significant difference between the two groups (L1- and L2-PRA groups), whereas the L1-PRA group valued PRAs significantly higher than the L2-PRA group with regard to the summary writing tests.

■ There was a significant association between the actual language use during PRAs and the participants' evaluation of their language use.

That is, the majority of the L1-PRA group (78%) preferred L1 use to L2 use (0%) during PRAs, whereas the L2-PRA group did not show such a clear preference for either the L1 or L2.

■ The participants of both groups showed a significantly strong preference for the L1 or the L2 depending on different circumstances of the L2 reading lesson. The L1 was preferred for the teacher explaining grammar rules or structures and making classroom announcements, while the L2 was preferred for the teacher providing answers to reading comprehension tests and asking questions as well as for students answering questions.

Based on the findings of the previous research, the researcher has reflected on why the different language use during the PRAs did not have a significant influence on the results of reading comprehension as she had expected. There seems to be several possible causes. First, the control of language use during the PRAs might not have been strict enough. Although the PRAs were conducted according to the specific questions focusing on three activities (listing, ranking, mapping), the content of participants' group discussion varied widely depending on their background knowledge on the topic and English proficiency level for the L2 group. This might have hindered the accurate measurement of influences of different language use during the PRAs on L2 reading. Second, the measurement tools of reading comprehension, which were reading comprehension tests (multiple-choice questions in English) and summary writing tests (fill-in-the-blank questions in Japanese), might not have accurately reflected the influences of the treatment. More specifically, the participants were able to see the text while taking the reading comprehension tests. This condition might have allowed the participants to merely process the text information superficially since they did not have to go through deep processing in order to store the information in their long term memory. If L1 use contributes to such deep processing, it is necessary to create a different type of measurement, such as a text-removed summary completion test. Third, the participants' level of English proficiency might have been too high to have benefitted from L1 use during the PRAs. If the level of participants had been lower, the experiment might have shown different results.

In terms of reading attitudes, however, the L1 group clearly favored the L1 over the L2 for the PRAs and valued the L1 significantly higher than the L2 for the summary writing tests. These results seem to indicate a certain benefit of L1-PRAs for the summary writing tests according to the participants' perception, which was not reflected on the scores of reading comprehension tests or summary writing tests. This led the researcher to develop more appropriate research design and instruments for the current study.

3. Hypotheses

Based on the literature review and the results of previous research, the following three hypotheses on language use during peer interaction for L2 reading have been formed.

1. L1 use during the peer interaction would facilitate cognitive processing and collaboration, resulting in better reading comprehension and memory retention compared to the case of L2 peer interaction.

2. L1 use during peer interaction in the form of pair work would facilitate interaction and enhance the quantity and quality of pair work outcomes; and also L1 pair work would be more appreciated by students as compared to L2 pair work.

3. Language preference, L1 or L2, would be influenced by students' L2 proficiency levels and circumstances of the lesson.

E. Research Questions

Based on the hypotheses described above, now the researcher will present the following five research questions (RQs) for examining the influences of language use on L2 reading.

RQ (1) Does the language use during the pair work (PW) influence the results of the summary completion test (ST) and the delayed summary completion test (DST); and does this influence vary depending on the English proficiency levels?

RQ (2) Does the language use during PW influence the PW production; and does this influence vary depending on the English proficiency levels?

RQ (3) Does the language use during PW influence the numerical and survey evaluation of PW; and does this influence vary depending on the English proficiency levels?

RQ (4) Does the language use during PW influence PW language preference and its survey evaluation; and does this influence vary depending on the English proficiency levels?

RQ (5) Do the different circumstances of the reading lesson influence the participants' language preference, L1 or L2?

RQ (1) explores the influences of language use during the pair work on reading comprehension gauged by the summary completion test and the delayed summary completion test. If there is a significant difference between the L1 and L2 groups, it indicates that either the L1 or L2 use during the pair work is more beneficial in terms of reading comprehension or memory retention. If there is no significant difference, on the other hand, it implies that either language can be used for the pair work flexibly according to students' proficiency level, the content of the class, or the purpose of the lesson. RQ (2) examines the results of pair-work production. If one of the languages promotes the pair work significantly, it can be said that either the L1 or L2 is more beneficial as a pair-work language than the other. RQ (3) explores how the pair work is evaluated in relation to the summary completion test. If either the L1 or L2 group evaluates the pair work significantly higher than the other group, it suggests that one of the languages is more suitable for conducting pair work according to the participants' perception. RQ (4) examines the pair-work language preference, that is, L1 preference, L2 preference, or no preference, and the preference reasons. If the pattern of language preference is significantly different between the L1 and L2 groups, the actual language use during the pair work seems to have an influence on their preference. RQ (5) explores how the research participants' language preference would vary according to different circumstances during the reading lesson in general. If one of the languages is preferred significantly more than the other at a certain occasion, it will provide useful information for the teacher to choose an appropriate language at difference circumstances during the lesson. In relation to the three hypotheses described above, RQ (1) will examine Hypothesis 1, research questions (2) and (3) will explore Hypothesis 2, and RQ (4) and (5) will test Hypothesis 3.

The detailed information about the research design to examine the research questions above will be explained in the following chapter.

Chapter III
The Study

The current study was designed to examine the influence of language use during pair work (PW) on L2 reading. The independent variable of the research, therefore, was the language use during PW, and the dependent variables were reading comprehension and reading attitudes. Reading comprehension was measured by a text-removed summary completion test (ST) and delayed summary completion test (DST). After reading the L2 text individually, the participants had PW, discussing seven focus questions in either the L1 or the L2, and answered ST with multiple-choice fill-in-the-blank questions. The same participants took DST (the same content as ST) a week later without referring to the text. During PW, four pairs chosen at random for the L1 group and for the L2 group, at both the upper-intermediate level and the novice level were audio-recorded. In order to examine participants' reading attitudes, a buffer task (BT) was held between the individual reading and PW. In addition, the post research questionnaire (PRSQ) was given to the participants after ST. All the data obtained were statistically analyzed in order to examine the influence of language use during PW on reading comprehension and reading attitudes. The research design of the current study is summarized in Table 1 on the following page in accordance with research questions, measurement tools, and methods of statistical analysis.

Table 1

Research design of the current study

Research questions (RQ)	Measurement tools	Method of statistical analysis
RQ (1) Does the language use during the pair work (PW) influence the results of the summary completion test (ST) and the delayed summary completion test (DST); and does this influence vary depending on the English proficiency levels?	ST and DST (21 multiple-choice questions)	ANOVA
RQ (2) Does the language use during PW influence the PW production; and does this influence vary depending on the English proficiency levels?	Scores of PW (7 written-answer focus questions)	t-test
RQ (3) Does the language use during PW influence the numerical and survey evaluation of PW; and does this influence vary depending on the English proficiency levels?	Post research questionnaire (#1 & #2)	t-test & descriptive analysis
RQ (4) Does the language use during PW influence PW language preference and its survey evaluation; and does this influence vary depending on the English proficiency levels?	Post research questionnaire (#3 & #4)	Chi-square test & descriptive analysis
RQ (5) Do the different occasions of the reading lesson influence the participants' language preference, L1 or L2?	Post research questionnaire (#5)	Chi-square test

Chapter III   The Study   *65*

A. Methods

1. Participants

The data of the current study were collected from two cohorts. One of them was made up of 61 female sophomores at the upper-intermediate level of English proficiency. Their majors were English literature (n = 56) and international relations (n = 5), and most of them were taking university English lessons four days a week. The other cohort was made up of 26 freshmen (8 males, 18 females) at the novice level of English proficiency. Their major was early childhood or primary education, and they were taking English lessons twice a week. Both groups were composed of Japanese university students who had undergone six years of English education at Japanese junior and senior high school. Ninety percent of the participants had no experience of studying or living abroad longer than three months. Since they were EFL students, they had limited English input and output outside the classroom. The difference between the two cohorts in terms of English proficiency levels was significant according to their TOEFL scores: t(85) = 16.01, p = .00. In fact, the highest range of novice-level scores was equal to the lowest range of upper-intermediate level scores, which showed very little overlap between the two cohorts. Moreover, the amount of exposure to English was apparently different between the two cohorts due to their majors and curricula. Therefore, instead of analyzing the two cohorts altogether, the researcher focused on data analysis within the two cohorts to reveal unique features that would differentiate the upper-intermediate and novice levels. These two cohorts were examined under the same research procedure at different periods of time. The experiment for the upper-intermediate cohort was conducted in July, 2014, while the experiment for the novice cohort was conducted in

January, 2015. All the experiments were conducted after the participants voluntarily signed the informed consent form (Appendix B).

Each cohort was divided into two subgroups at random to examine the influence of language use during the pair work (PW) on their reading comprehension and reading attitudes; one subgroup used Japanese (L1-PW) and the other subgroup used English (L2-PW) for their PW. In terms of regarding English proficiency, there was no significant difference between the two subgroups for each level. In other words, the only difference between the two subgroups was the language use during PW; the rest of the lesson was conducted in English following the exactly the same procedures. The participants of the current study are summarized in Table 2 below.

Table 2

The participants

	L1-PW	L2-PW	Total
Upper-intermediate level			
Number of participants	n = 31	n = 30	N = 61
Mean of TOEFL PBT	508.48	499.36	503.92
SD	33.19	25.87	29.53
Minimum-Maximum scores	423-587	450-562	423-587
Differences between the groups	$t(59) = 1.19, p = .23$ (n.s.)		
Novice level			
Number of participants	n = 14	n = 12	N = 26
Mean of TOEFL PBT	399.77	403.01	401.39
SD	20.24	20.54	20.39
Minimum-Maximum scores	360-426	370-433	360-433
Differences between the groups	$t(24) = .40, p = .69$ (n.s.)		

Note: A junior student participated in the upper-intermediate level in order to make a pair during PW. The person's score was excluded from the L1-PW group to maintain its consistency.

2. Data collection instruments

In order to measure the influence of language use during PW on reading comprehension and reading attitudes, the researcher developed the following four instruments: (a) text-removed summary completion test (ST) and delayed summary completion test (DST), (b) buffer task (BT), (c) pair work (PW) focus questions, and (d) post-research questionnaire (PRSQ). These instruments were developed and modified based on the results of the pre-pilot test and pilot test. Each test was conducted during a six-month or three-month period prior to the main data collection.

Except PRSQ, which was adopted from the previous research (Matsumoto, 2013), all of the other instruments originate from Taylor's (2013) well-designed research on reading summary tasks. A detailed description of her research can be found in Appendix C. Since the validity and reliability of the instruments created by Taylor had been already examined, they seemed suitable for the purpose of the current study. According to her research, the summary completion task has been proven as an accurate measurement of reading comprehension. Therefore, it is possible to examine how the language use during PW, namely, discussing focus questions to elicit essential information, would influence the results of reading comprehension and reading attitudes. For the reasons described above, the researcher decided to adopt from Taylor's research one of the reading texts, a text-removed summary completion task, and probe questions, which are called focus questions in the current study. As mentioned earlier, these adopted instruments were revised several times according to the results of the pre-pilot and pilot studies. Each instrument will be explained in detail in the following section.

a. Text-removed summary completion test (ST) and delayed summary completion test (DST) (Appendices E & F)

The reading text for the summary completion test was a short exposition (a 389-word newspaper editorial on anorexia: Appendix D). The text consisted of the following lexical items: 82.95% of the vocabulary was categorized as belonging to the 2,000 most common word families, 5.60% was recognized as academic words, and 11.45% was off-list words (according to *Web VP Classis* by Cobb, n.d.). In Taylor's research, the students (170 mixed-level students aged 13−14) were asked to provide written responses to fill in 39 blanks on the summary completion task (Taylor, 2013, p.236). The results were as follows: mean score = 12.87 (out of 39), SD = 8.25, the internal consistency = .88 (Rash analysis). In spite of the fact that the readers were all native speakers of English, the mean score appears to be rather low (the ratio of correct answer = 33%). Based on these results, the researcher assumed that it would be even more difficult for average Japanese university students to produce written responses on the same task. Hence, the researcher modified the original task into a multiple choice (four alternatives each) summary completion test (ST). In addition, an English-Japanese glossary was attached to the reading text regarding 16 lexical items, which would possibly interfere with comprehension. In light of the focus of the current research, that is, examining the influence of language use during PW, unrelated variables, such as vocabulary knowledge or L2 writing skills, needed to be eliminated. All the alternatives for each question and the definition of each lexical item on the glossary were examined carefully and revised with the cooperation of three other SLA researchers.

This modified version of ST was tested on four Japanese graduate students whose major was English teaching. Their mean score was 23.75 (out of 39) and the ratio of correct answers was 60.90%. All of the students claimed, however, that the number of questions was overwhelming. Therefore, the researcher reduced the number of questions from 39 to 21 by limiting roughly one question per sentence. This revised ST was tested on two graduate students whose major was also English teaching, and their mean score was 13.5 (out of 21) and the ratio of correct answer was 64.29%. According to their feedback, the number of questions was acceptable. This is how the summary completion test was developed prior to the pilot study, and it was further modified according to the results of the pilot study. The finalized version of the summary completion test can be found in Appendix E.

The content of DST (Appendix F) was generally identical to that of ST. The only difference between them was the timing: DST was conducted one week after ST. The pre-pilot study did not include DST since it was conducted to check the format and content of the summary completion test, not to compare the results between ST and DST.

b. Buffer task (BT) (Appendix G)

According to Taylor (2013), the purpose of having a buffer task (BT) prior to a recall task is to examine readers' mental representations constructed in their long-term memory (p.87). In other words, the time lag between text reading and the recall task requires that readers access the long-term memory in which the processed text information is stored. To be stored in the long-term memory, mental representations, namely, "situation model" in Kintsch's term, constructed during and after text reading, need to undergo deep cognitive processing. Since the researcher hypothesized that L1 use during PW would facilitate deeper cognitive processing compared to L2-PW, it was necessary to conduct BT prior to PW and ST for the current study.

BT asked the participants the following six questions in Japanese: (a) the participants' name; (b) year and major; (c) TOEFL score; (d) experience of living or studying abroad including location, length of stay, and type of educational institution; (e) evaluation of the reading text's difficulty with a five-point Likert scale; and (f) the amount of background information regarding the reading topic again with a five-point Likert scale. The first three questions were to identify each of the participants and their proficiency levels. The third question was asked to eliminate any participant with outstanding background of English study or experiences in an English-speaking environment, which would have disturbed the consistency of the participant groups. The last two questions were to compare the pre-condition of L1 and L2 PW-groups. The questions examined the participants' evaluation of text difficulty and the amount of background knowledge on the topic. The data obtained from the last two questions were analyzed by a t-test.

c. Pair work (PW) focus questions (Appendix H)

The seven questions were adopted from Taylor's probe questions for eliciting oral recall (2013, p.224). The current research called these PW focus questions, which asked key factors needed to be included in the summary. For the L1-PW group, all the questions were written in Japanese and the participants needed to provide their written responses in Japanese based on their Japanese discussion. Likewise, the members of the L2-PW group were provided with English questions and asked to respond to them in English based on their English discussion. Both groups were required to do PW under the text-removed condition. This condition was set in order to facilitate participants' text recall that accessed long-term memory.

The written responses were graded by three graders: two graduate students majoring teaching English and the researcher. The inter-rater reliability was 83.36%, and the disagreements of grading were solved by discussion among the graders. For the grading, the researcher created the

Chapter III   The Study   *71*

answer key (Appendix I) in both languages, based on Taylor's summary completion task answer key (2013, pp.237–238). The model answers for each question included two to four propositions and each proposition deserved a point. That is, even if a pair was not able to produce a complete answer or a grammatically correct sentence, they were given partial points accordingly. Since the purpose of the current study was not to measure the participants' writing skills, the researcher focused on the number of propositions that they could recall during PW. The total score was 18 points and the result of PW was analyzed via a t-test in order to examine if there was a significant difference between the L1 and L2 PW groups.

In addition to the written responses to PW focus questions, the researcher also audio-recorded peer interaction of four randomly chosen pairs for each level and in each L1 and L2-PW group (4 pairs x 2 levels x 2 PW-groups = 16 recordings in total). These recordings were transcribed by the researcher for the purpose of eliciting certain patterns of peer interaction that could be unique to one of the proficiency levels or PW-groups. The obtained data were used to indicate some examples of peer interaction.

d. Post-research questionnaire (PRSQ) (Appendix J)

The PRSQ consisted of five questions adopted from the previous research (Matsumoto, 2013). All the questions were multiple-choice and written in Japanese to avoid the influence of L2 language skills. The PRSQ (1) asked the participants to evaluate PW. They chose an answer out of the following four alternatives. That is, PW was either (a) useful, (b) relatively useful, (c) relatively useless, or (d) useless. The answers with a four-point Likert scale were assigned for five, four, two, or one point(s) respectively for the purpose of statistical analysis (t-test).

In the PRSQ (2), the participants were asked to choose a reason from the given lists regarding their PW evaluation in PRSQ (1). There were two kinds of lists for PRSQ (2). The first was for those who answered with the positive evaluation of "useful" or "relatively useful" in PRSQ (1). The second was for those who answered with negative evaluation of "relatively useless" and "useless" in PRSQ (1). Each list of reasons (5 alternatives) was modified from the previous research (Matsumoto, 2013). The five alternative reasons for positive PW evaluation are summarized as follows. The participants evaluated PW positively because they were (a) able to share background knowledge, (b) able to understand the theme or main ideas, (c) able to understand the details, (d) able to understand the vocabulary, or (e) for other reason. The five alternative reasons for negative PW evaluation are summarized as follows. The participants evaluated PW negatively because they were (f) unable to share background knowledge, (g) unable to understand the theme or main ideas, (h) unable to understand the details, (i) unable to understand the vocabulary, or (j) for other reason. The obtained data were analyzed descriptively.

The PRSQ (3) was about PW language preference, and the participants were asked to choose one response out of the following three alternatives: (a) L1 (Japanese) preference, (b) L2 (English) preference, or (c) no preference. The results were analyzed by a chi-square test.

In relation to the third question, the PRSQ (4) required the participants to choose a reason for their PW language preference out of twelve alternatives. These alternatives were elicited from the written responses in the pilot study and coded into twelve categories by three raters who were familiar with the coding system. The twelve alternatives are summarized as follows. Participants chose a certain PW language for (a) interacting smoothly, (b) filling in the gap of L2 linguistic knowledge, (c) sharing details, (d) thinking deeply, (e) enhancing text comprehension, (f) dealing with a difficult topic, (g) exchanging information efficiently,

Chapter III   The Study   *73*

(h) minimizing thinking time, (i) using the same language as text and ST, (j) recalling the text information efficiently, (k) practicing the language, or for (l) some other reason. The participants' responses were analyzed descriptively.

The previous four questions (PRSQs [1]-[4]) were designed to examine if there were any significant differences between L1 and L2 PW groups. In contrast, the PRSQ (5) was intended to collect Japanese university students' general opinions regardless of experimental conditions or proficiency levels. Therefore, the question referred to the general situation of English classroom. The participants were asked their language preference, whether L1 or L2, in eight different circumstances during the reading lesson as follows: (a) when the teacher is explaining vocabulary, (b) when the teacher is explaining grammar rules and structure, (c) when the teacher is providing answers to reading comprehension test (RCT), (d) when the teacher is explaining the answers of RCT, (e) when the teacher is asking students questions, (f) when the teacher is making classroom announcements, (g) when students are answering questions from the teacher, and (h) when students are having a discussion. The purpose of PRSQ (5) was to examine if there were any significant patterns of language preference in accordance with different circumstances of the reading lesson described above. In order to collect as much data as possible, the researcher included all the data obtained from those who participated in the first session of the experiment, even though some of them were not able to take DST. This was the reason why the total number of participants for the PRSQ (5) was different from other data.

To summarize, all the research instruments described above were designed carefully based on the well-developed Taylor's study (2013) and previous research (Matsumoto, 2013). These instruments were revised several times in order to enhance the quality of measurement.

The current study focused on quantitative data, with the intention of conducting a feasible yet reliable data analysis. In the following section, the experimental procedures using these research instruments will be described.

3. Experimental procedures

There were six steps for the first session of the experiment: (a) preparation, (b) individual reading of the text, (c) buffer task [BT], (d) pair work [PW], (e) summary completion test [ST], and (f) post-research questionnaire [PRSQ]. In addition, the delayed summary completion test [DST] was conducted one week later. The participants were not previously informed of the delayed summary completion test, and they had no access to the reading text. Therefore, there was little possibility for them to review the content of the reading between the first experiment and the delayed summary completion test. Each step is summarized in Table 3 below.

Table 3

Six steps of experimental procedure

(a) Preparation (5 min.):
● Eachcohort (upper-intermediate and novice level) was divided into two types of PW-groups (L1 or L2) at random.
● The L1-PW group was seated on the right side of the classroom and the L2-PW group was on the left side, with an open space between the two groups.
● The researcher explained the purpose and procedure of the experiment briefly in English, and the participants voluntarily signed the informed consent form.
● Research assistants distributed and collected handouts, facilitated PW, and operated IC recorders.
(b) Individual reading (15 min.):
● The reading text was distributed and the participants read it individually without consulting a dictionary.
● The reading text was collected after the reading.

Chapter III   The Study   75

(c) Buffer task (5 min.):
● The participants answered the questions in Japanese individually.

(d) Pair work (35 min.):
● The participants were asked to make pairs with the person next to them.
● The package of PW focus questions (one question was printed on each page: total seven pages) was distributed to each pair.
● Roughly four minutes was allocated to discuss each focus question in pairs: the researcher announced the time to start or stop each question so that all the pairs would follow the same pace. The L1-PW group used Japanese and the L2-PW group used English for their PW and provided written responses in each language.
● The 16 pairs chosen at random (4 pairs x 2 levels x 2 types of PW-groups) were recorded their interaction during PW.

(e) Text-removed summary completion test (15 min.):
● The participants answered 21 multiple-choice questions on ST individually.

(f) Post-research questionnaire (5 min.):
● The participants answered five questions in Japanese individually.

⟨One-week later⟩

Delayed summary completion test (15 min.):
● The participants took DST individually without consulting the reading text or a dictionary.

Note: For the upper-intermediate level, the number of participants decreased from ST (n = 77) to DST (n = 61). Therefore, the data obtained from those who took both ST and DST were used for all the statistical analysis, except the PRSQ (5). For the novice level, the number of the participants was the same on ST and DST (n = 26).

It took about 85 minutes to conduct the first session of the experiment and 15 minutes for DST. As explained previously, the only difference between L1 and L2 groups was the language use during PW. The rest of the experiment was conducted in English by the researcher in cooperation with research assistants.

4. Data analysis tools

In order to examine differences between L1 and L2 PW groups regarding their reading comprehension and reading attitudes, the following statistical analysis was conducted. First, two-way mixed analysis of variance (ANOVA) was computed to analyze the results of ST and DST. The inter-subject factor was the types of groups, namely, the L1-PW group and the L2-PW group. The intra-subject factor, on the other hand, was the types of tests, that is, ST and DST. Second, the scores of PW focus questions were analyzed via a t-test to examine the difference between the two PW-groups. Third, in order to investigate the influence of language use during PW on participants' evaluation of PW, a t-test was conducted for the PRSQ (1), where responses to a four-point Likert scale were converted into numerical scale. Fourth, Pearson's chi-square was used for the PRSQ (3) in order to examine the correlations between the actual language use during PW and participants' preference of PW language. Pearson's chi-square was also used for the PRSQ (5) in order to analyze participants' language preference at eight different circumstances during the general reading lesson. The participants' survey evaluations of PW and PW language preference (PRSQs, [2] and [4]) were analyzed descriptively. In addition, the participants' evaluation of text difficulty and the background knowledge about the reading topic (BT [4] and [5]) were analyzed using a t-test. All the statistical analysis was computed by the SPSS ver. 22.0. An alpha level of .05 was used for all the statistical tests. Due to the repeated measurements, however, the alpha level was adjusted according to Bonferroni's correction as follows: For PRSQ (5), the alpha level was .00625, i.e., .05 divided by 8. The effect size of each statistical analysis was calculated as follows: Cohen's d and η^2 were based on the formulas that Mizumoto and Takeuchi suggested (2008, p.50) and η_p^2 and Cramer's V were according to SPSS ver. 22.0.

5. Pilot study

A pilot study was conducted three months prior to the current study. The detailed description of the pilot study and its revising process for the main data collection will be found in Appendix K. Through the revisions, the instruments for the main data collection were fine-tuned and prepared.

B. Results

In this section, the researcher will describe the results of statistical analysis on the data obtained from the experiment related to the research questions (RQs) (1) through (5).

1. Research Question (1): Influence of language use on reading comprehension

RQ (1) explored the influences of language use during the pair work (PW) on reading comprehension, that is, the results of summary completion test [ST] and delayed summary completion test [DST], for two different proficiency levels (upper-intermediate and novice). In order to examine the data, a two-way mixed ANOVA was computed. Within the upper-intermediate level, the ANOVA showed no significant main effect regarding types of PW groups (L1 and L2 PW groups): $F(1, 59) = .10$, $p = .74$, $\eta^2 = .00$ ($\eta_p^2 = .00$). The interaction between the types of groups and the types of tests (ST and DST) was not significant, $F(1, 59) = 3.41$, $p = .07$, $\eta^2 = .05$ ($\eta_p^2 = .05$). In contrast, within the novice-level, the interaction between the two factors was significant: $F (1, 24) = 9.77$, $p = .00$, $\eta^2 = .26$ ($\eta_p^2 = .28$). Since a cross-over interaction was observed, tests of simple main effects were conducted. The simple main effect of PW groups, i.e., L1 and L2 PW groups, was not significant either on ST: $F(1, 24) = 3.28$, $p = .08$ or on DST: $F(1, 24) = 2.46$, $p = .13$. On the other hand, the simple main effect of tests (ST and DST) was significant within the L2-PW group: $F(1, 24) = 11.84, p = .00$. That is, the L2-PW group score on DST significantly dropped compared to ST score ($9.58 \rightarrow 6.58$). Meanwhile, the L1-PW group did not indicate any significant difference between ST and DST: $F(1, 24) = .78, p = .38$.

Although not at a statistically significant level, the score of the novice-level L1-PW group even increased from ST to DST ($7.64 \rightarrow 8.35$). The same phenomenon was observed for the upper-intermediate level, where the L1-PW group increased their scores from ST to DST ($14.87 \rightarrow 15.09$). Although it is necessary to bear in mind that there was no significant difference between the L1-PW and L2-PW groups, these results seem to indicate some relation between the pair-work language use and long-term memory, especially for the novice level.

Regarding the above argument, there is an important aspect that needed to be explained. That is, the L2-PW group at the novice level obtained a slightly higher score on ST compared to the L1-PW group ($9.58 > 7.64$), though not at a statistically significant level. The difference between the scores of the two groups, however, was probably a reflection of their background knowledge on the topic. The results of the buffer task (BT) revealed the amount of background knowledge that the L2-PW group reported to have exceeded that of the L1-PW group significantly at the novice level: $t(24) = 2.29, p = .03$, Cohen's $d = .90$. On the other hand, the upper-intermediate level did not show any significant difference between the L1 and L2 groups in this regard: $t(59) = .17, p = .86$, Cohen's $d = .04$. In addition, the results of BT question examining the text difficulty perceived by the participants did not indicate any significant difference between the groups at either level: the upper-intermediate level, $t(59) = .22, p = .82$, Cohen's $d = .06$; the novice level, $t(24) = .97, p = .33$, Cohen's $d = .38$. Despite the fact that the novice-level L2-PW group had

Chapter III   The Study   79

the advantage of background knowledge, they were not able to sustain it until DST, where the L1-PW group surpassed in the scores (6.58 < 8.35). The researcher will examine this aspect further in the Discussion section later. The results of RQ (1) are summarized in Tables 4 and 5 below.

Table 4

Descriptive Statistics and Two-way Mixed ANOVA Summary Tables on ST and DST
Descriptive Statistics on ST and DST for Upper-intermediate Level

Group		ST	DST	Mean
L1-PW group (n = 31)	Mean	14.87	15.09	14.98
	SD	3.24	3.00	3.12
L2-PW group (n = 30)	Mean	15.10	14.40	14.75
	SD	2.41	2.98	2.69
Total (N = 61)	Mean	14.98	14.75	14.86
	SD	2.84	2.99	2.91

Two-way Mixed ANOVA Summary Table on ST and DST for Upper-intermediate Level

Source	SS	df	MS	F	p	η^2 (η_p^2)
Between Groups						
Group (L1 or L2)	1.66	1	1.66	.10	.74	.00 (.00)
Error	901.23	59	15.27	—	—	—
Within Groups						
Test (ST &DST)	1.71	1	1.71	.89	.34	.01 (.01)
Test x Group	6.53	1	6.53	3.41	.07	.05 (.05)
Error	112.86	59	1.91	—	—	—
Total	1023.99	121	—	—	—	—

Note: The full point of ST and DST was 21 points.

Table 5

Descriptive Statistics and Two-way Mixed ANOVA Summary Tables on ST and DST

Descriptive Statistics on ST and DST for Novice Level

Group		ST	DST	Mean
L1-PW group (n = 14)	Mean	7.64	8.35	7.99
	SD	2.87	2.34	2.60
L2-PW group (n = 12)	Mean	9.58	6.58	8.08
	SD	2.53	3.39	2.96
Total (N = 26)	Mean	8.53	7.53	8.03
	SD	2.84	2.95	2.89

Two-way Mixed ANOVA Summary Table on ST and DST for Novice Level

Source	SS	df	MS	F	p	η^2 (η_p^2)
Between Groups						
Group (L1 or L2)	.09	1	.09	.00	.92	.00 (.00)
Error	266.83	24	11.11	–	–	–
Within Groups						
Test (ST &DST)	16.87	1	16.87	3.70	.06	.10 (.13)
Test x Group	44.57	1	44.57	9.77	.00**	.26 (.28)
Error	109.42	24	4.56	–	–	–
Total	437.78	51	–	–	–	–

**$p < .01$

2. Research Question (2): Influence of language use on the outcomes of pair work

RQ (2) examined the results of pair work (PW) production based on the graded scores of seven focus questions. The results of t-test analysis showed that within the upper-intermediate level, the L1-PW group (19 pairs) obtained a significantly higher score than the L2-PW group (20 pairs): $t(37) = 3.99$, $p = .00$, Cohen's $d = 1.28$. Likewise, within the novice-level, the L1-PW group (7 pairs) obtained a significantly higher score than the L2-PW group (6 pairs): $t(11) = 2.45$, $p = .03$, Cohen's $d =$

1.37. These results clearly showed that L1-PW influenced the scores of PW production positively for both upper-intermediate and novice levels. The results of RQ (2) are summarized in Table 6 below.

Table 6

Descriptive Statistics and t-test Summary Tables on PW
t-test Results Comparing L1-PW Group and L2-PW group on PW for Upper-intermediate Level

PW	Mean	SD	t	df	p	Effect size (Cohen's d)
L1-PW (n = 19)	11.10	2.51	–	–	–	–
L2-PW (n = 20)	8.00	2.33	–	–	–	–
Total	9.55	2.42	3.99	37	.00**	1.28

**$p<.01$

t-test Results Comparing L1-PW Group and L2-PW group on PW for Novice Level

PW	Mean	SD	t	df	p	Effect size (Cohen's d)
L1-PW (n = 7)	7.14	1.95	–	–	–	–
L2-PW (n = 6)	4.66	1.63	–	–	–	–
Total	5.90	1.79	2.45	11	.03*	1.37

*$p<.05$

3. Research Question (3): Influence of language use on pair-work evaluation

RQ (3) explored how the participants evaluated PW in relation to ST. The data were collected via PRSQs (1) and (2). First, PRSQ (1) examined PW evaluation numerically. The participants were asked to evaluate how useful PW was for ST, and to choose one of the following four alternatives: (a) useful, (b) relatively useful, (c) relatively useless, or (d) useless. Each answer was converted into numerical data and a t-test was computed in order to see if there was any differences between the L1 and L2 PW groups. The upper-intermediate level did not show any significant difference between the groups: $t(59) = .70$, $p = .48$, Cohen's $d = .19$. In contrast, the novice level showed a significant difference between the groups. That is, the L1-PW group valued PW significantly higher than the L2-PW group: $t(13.52) = 2.15$, $p = .04$, Cohen's $d = .91$. Considering the generally limited L2 language skills at the novice level, it is natural that the L1-PW group valued PW much higher than the L2-PW group. Moreover, as described in the previous section (RQ [2]), the L1-PW groups obtained significantly higher scores on PW focus questions for both novice and upper-intermediate levels. This result shows how effective L1-PW was in terms of PW production for both levels, and in particular, the novice participants appreciated L1-PW much more than L2-PW.

To summarize the results of RQ (3), PW was valued significantly higher by the L1-PW group than by the L2-PW group at the novice level, whereas there was not such a difference between the groups at the upper-intermediate level. The results of numerical PW evaluation are shown in Table 7 on the following page.

Table 7

Descriptive Statistics and t-test Summary Tables on Numerical PW Evaluation
Descriptive Statistics and t-test Summary Table on Numerical PW Evaluation for
Upper-intermediate Level

PW	Mean	SD	t	df	p	Effect size (Cohen's d)
L1-PW (n = 31)	4.35	.79	–	–	–	–
L2-PW (n = 30)	4.50	.82	–	–	–	–
Total	4.42	.80	.70	59	.48	.19

Descriptive Statistics and t-test Summary Table on Numerical PW Evaluation for
Novice Level

PW	Mean	SD	t	df	p	Effect size (Cohen's d)
L1-PW (n = 14)	4.64	.49	–	–	–	–
L2-PW (n = 12)	3.75	1.35	–	–	–	–
Total	4.19	.92	2.15	13.52	.04*	.91

*p < .05

In relation to the numerical PW evaluation above, the participants also responded to the survey evaluation via PRSQ (2), where they chose a reason for their PW evaluation out of five alternatives according to their responses (positive or negative) on PRSQ (1). For instance, if a participant considered PW to be useful or relatively useful, he or she chose one response from the list of the following positive reasons: (a) being able to share background knowledge; (b) being able to understand the theme or main ideas; (c) being able to understand details; (d) being able to understand vocabulary; or (e) other. On the other hand, if a participant

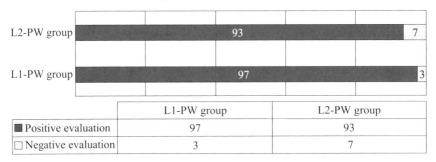

Figure 6. Results of pair-work evaluation for upper-intermediate level. According to the response on PRSQ (1), positive evaluation (useful or relatively useful) is shown in black and negative evaluation (useless or relatively useless) is shown in gray.

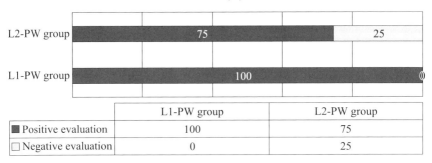

Figure 7. Results of pair-work evaluation for novice level. According to the response on PRSQ (1), positive evaluation (useful or relatively useful) is shown in black and negative evaluation (useless or relatively useless) is shown in gray.

evaluated PW as useless or relatively useless, the reason for the evaluation was chosen from the list of negative reasons: (f) being unable to share background knowledge; (g) being unable to understand the theme or main ideas; (h) being unable to understand details; (i) being unable to understand vocabulary; or (j) other. Since the obtained data needed to

Chapter III   The Study   *85*

be examined according to the responses on PRSQ (1), the researcher summarized the results of the question (positive or negative evaluation of PW) descriptively for each level in Figures 6 and 7 on the previous page.

As Figures 6 and 7 indicate, the percentage of positive PW evaluations for both levels was extremely high. For the upper-intermediate level, 97% of the L1-PW group and 93% of the L2-PW group showed positive evaluations. Within the novice level, 100% of the L1-PW group and 75% of the L2-PW group showed positive evaluations. According to the results, PW seemed to be valued positively by the vast majority of participants regardless of PW language use or levels. There was, however, a noticeable difference between L1 and L2 PW groups for the novice level. Compared to the 100% positive evaluations of the L1-PW group, the L2-PW group showed relatively lower percentage of positive evaluations (75%). In other words, the L2-PW group was not as satisfied with their PW as their counterpart, that is, L1-PW group.

The results of survey evaluation of PW are summarized in Figure 8 on the following page. Since the vast majority of participants valued PW positively, the researcher will first describe the reasons for positive evaluations and then present the negative evaluations.

According to Figure 8, the common reasons for positive PW evaluation were "being able to understand the theme or main ideas" and " being able to share background knowledge" regardless of PW language use or levels. On the other hand, there were differences between the levels regarding the following two aspects. One difference was that the upper-intermediate level indicated the reason "being able to understand details" for their positive PW evaluation, whereas the novice level did not. The other difference was that nearly one-third of novice level participants chose the reason, "being able to share background knowledge" for positive PW evaluation, whereas the percentage of the

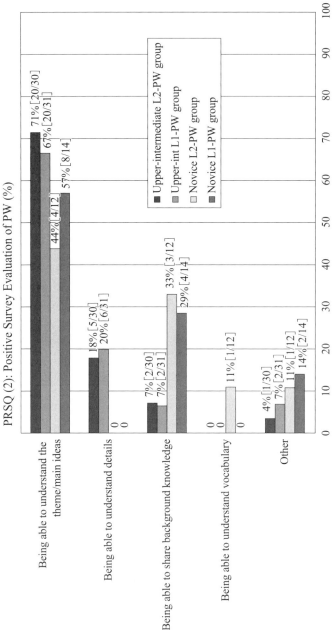

Figure 8. Positive pair-work survey evaluation by the L1 and L2 pair-work groups for upper-intermediate and novice levels. The five reasons for positive evaluation are listed above along with the percentage for each reason within each of the four groups. The percentage is calculated by dividing the number of responses by the total number of positive survey evaluations within the same group. The numbers in the square brackets indicate: [the number of responses / the total number of participants in the same group].

upper-intermediate who chose the same reason was relatively small (7%). The researcher will discuss possible explanations for these differences later in the Discussion section.

The number of negative PW evaluations, on the other hand, was very limited. The ratio of such negative evaluations are as follows: 3% of the L1-PW group and 7% of the L2-PW group within the upper-intermediate level; 0% of the L1-PW group and 25% of the L2-PW group within the novice level. For the upper-intermediate level, both L1 and L2 PW groups had one participant who chose "being unable to understand details" as a reason for a negative PW evaluation. Another participant

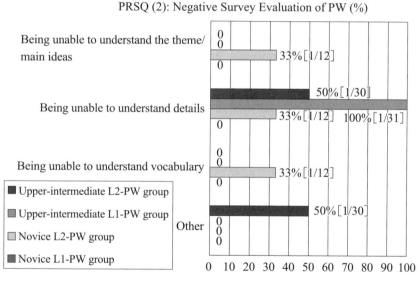

Figure 9. Negative pair-work survey evaluation by the L1 and L2 pair-work groups for upper-intermediate and novice levels. The four reasons for negative evaluation are listed above along with the percentage for each reason within each of the four groups. The percentage is calculated by dividing the number of responses by the total number of negative survey evaluations within the same group. The numbers in the square brackets indicate: [the number of responses / the total number of participants in the same group].

of the L2-PW group chose "other." Within the novice level, the L1-PW group showed no negative PW evaluation. In contrast, three participants of L2-PW group indicated the following three reasons for their negative PW evaluation: "being unable to understand the theme or main ideas," "being unable to understand details," and "being unable to understand the vocabulary." These results are summarized in Figure 9 on the previous page. A cautious interpretation is necessary for Figure 9, however, since the percentage of each response appears much larger due to the fact that the number of each response is divided by the total number of negative survey evaluation, which was rather small.

To summarize the results of RQ (3), the vast majority of participants evaluated PW positively regardless of PW language use or proficiency levels. The reasons for positive evaluation were similar between the upper-intermediate and novice levels. One exception, however, was that only the upper-intermediate level chose the reason "being able to understand details" for their positive PW evaluation. A very limited number of participants showed negative evaluations of PW. The interpretation of these results will be explained later in the Discussion section.

4. Research Question (4): Influence of language use on language preference for pair work

RQ (4) examined PW language preference (PRSQ [3]) and the preference reasons, using a survey evaluation (PRSQ [4]). First, the participants chose one response out of the following three alternatives to indicate their preference for PW language: (a) L1 preference, (b) L2 preference, or (c) no preference. The obtained data were analyzed by a chi-square test. The results indicated that for the upper-intermediate level, there was a significant difference between L1 and L2 PW groups in terms

Chapter III   The Study   *89*

Table 8

Descriptive Statistics and Chi-square Test Summary Table for PRSQ (3):
PW Language Preference x PW-groups (L1 and L2) for Upper-intermediate Level

	PW language preference			Total
	L1 preference	No preference	L2 preference	
L1-PW group				
Count	27	3	1	31
% within group	87.1%	9.7%	3.2%	
Adjusted standardized residual	3.8	-2.5	-2.3	
L2-PW group				
Count	12	11	7	30
% within group	40.0%	36.7%	23.3%	
Adjusted standardized residual	-3.8	2.5	2.3	
Total	39	14	8	61
Chi-square	$\chi^2(2) = 14.82, p = .00$**, Cramer's V = .49			

** $p < .01$

Descriptive Statistics and Chi-square Test Summary Table for PRSQ (3):
PW Language Preference x PW-groups (L1 and L2) for Novice Level

	PW language preference			Total
	L1 preference	No preference	L2 preference	
L1-PW group				
Count	9	4	1	14
% within group	64.3%	28.6%	7.1%	
Adjusted standardized residual	-2.3	2.0	.9	
L2-PW group				
Count	12	0	0	12
% within group	100%	0%	0%	
Adjusted standardized residual	2.3	-2.0	-.9	
Total	21	4	1	26
Chi-square	$\chi^2(2) = 5.30, p = .07$, Cramer's V = .45			

of their responses: $\chi^2(2, N=61) = 14.82, p = .00$, Cramer's V = .49. That is, the proportions of PW language preference was significantly different between the L1 and L2 PW groups. In contrast, the novice level did not show any significant difference between the groups: $\chi^2(2, N=26) = 5.30$, $p = .07$, Cramer's V = .45. The results of PRSQ (3) are summarized in Table 8 on the previous page.

The L1-PW group at the upper-intermediate level showed a clear preference for L1 use compared to L2 use during PW, i.e., 87% vs. 3%. On the other hand, the L2-PW group did not indicate such a clear preference either for the L1 (40%) or for the L2 (23%). In addition, about one-third of the participants (37%) did not sense much difference between L1 and L2 uses. These results suggest the following two points. The first point is that even for the upper-intermediate students, whose linguistic level seemed sufficient to conduct L2-PW, the L1-PW group showed strong preference for the L1. The second finding is that, in contrast, if the participants were encouraged to have L2-PW, they were capable of doing so without having much language difficulty. This explains why the L2-PW group did not show a clear preference for the L1 as described above. Meanwhile, for the novice level, the majority of the L1-PW group (64%)

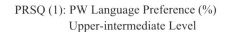
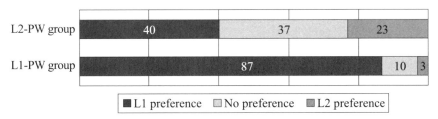

Figure 10. Percentage of pair-work language preference in L1 and L2 pair-work groups within the upper-intermediate level.

Chapter III   The Study   *91*

PRSQ (3): PW Language Preference (%)
Novice Level

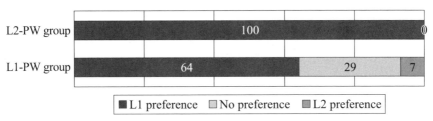

Figure 11. Percentage of pair-work language preference in L1 and L2 pair-work groups within the novice level.

showed L1 preference for PW. Moreover, all the participants (100%) of the L2-PW group were in favor of the L1 during PW. The results of descriptive analysis of PRSQ (3) are summarized in Figures 10 and 11 on the previous page.

In relation to the PW language preference above, participants were asked to take the survey evaluation of PW language preference, in which they chose one response, namely, a reason for PW language preference,

PRSQ (4): Survey Evaluation of PW Langauge Preference (%)
for Upper-intermediate Level

L1-PW group preferring L1 [27/31] for:

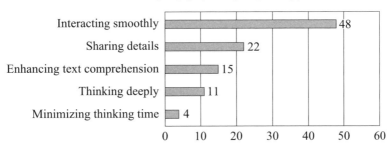

Figure 12. Reasons of L1 preference chosen by the upper-intermediate level L1 pair-work group. There are five reasons listed on the left. The number of response is shown in square brackets as [the number of response divided by the total number of participants] above in the bar graph.

out of twelve alternatives (PRSQ [4]). As explained previously, these alternatives were elicited from the pilot study via a coding system. The results of descriptive analysis were summarized according to their PW language preference, that is, L1, L2, or no preference, for each level and each PW-group. The data for the upper-intermediate level are shown in Figures 12-15, and the data for the novice level are described in Figures 16 and 17. Since the percentage is very small, the data will be described separately from the figures, including both the data of those who preferred the L2 or showed no preference within the upper-intermediate level and the data of those who preferred the L2 within the novice level.

According to Figure 12, the upper-intermediate level L1-PW group chose the first and fifth reasons, that is, 48%: interacting smoothly; 4%: minimizing thinking time, related to the efficiency of communication. The other three reasons, which are 22%: sharing details; 15%: enhancing text comprehension; 11%: thinking deeply, can be categorized as factors to enhance the depth of reading. Among the same group, only one

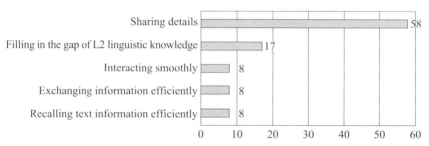

Figure 13. Reasons of L1 preference chosen by the upper-intermediate level L2 pair-work group. There are five reasons listed on the left. The number of response is shown in square brackets as [the number of response divided by the total number of participants] above in the bar graph.

Chapter III The Study 93

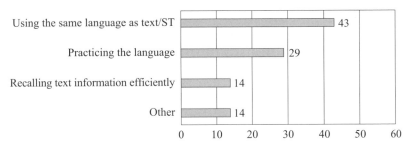

Figure 14. Reasons of L2 preference chosen by the upper-intermediate level L2 pair-work group. There are four reasons listed on the left. The number of response is shown in square brackets as [the number of response divided by the total number of participants] above in the bar graph.

participant preferred the L2 for the reason of using the same language as text and ST. In addition, three participants showed no preference for other reasons not included on the list.

Figure 13 shows that the majority of L2-PW group (nearly 59%) preferred the L1 for sharing details. The following three reasons, 17% for filling in the gap of L2 linguistic knowledge, 8% for interacting smoothly, and 8% for exchanging information efficiently, seem to be related to the efficiency of communication. Considering the fact that these L2-PW participants showed a desire to use the L1 for PW, these reasons seem to reflect their regret that more detailed information might have been shared had L1 use been allowed.

Figure 14 shows the reasons of L2 preference chosen by the L2-PW group for the upper-intermediate level. These reasons seem to be related to metalinguistic or metacognitive awareness as the following figures indicate: 43% using the same language as text and ST, 29% practicing the language, and 14% recalling text information efficiently. Such awareness,

PRSQ (4): Survey Evaluation of PW Language Preference (%) for Upper-intermediate Level

L2-PW group showing no preference [11/30] for:

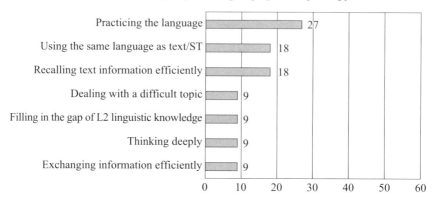

Figure 15. Reasons of no preference chosen by the upper-intermediate level L2 pair-work group. There are seven reasons listed on the left. The number of response is shown in square brackets as [the number of response divided by the total number of participants] above in the bar graph.

PRSQ (4): Survey Evaluation of PW Language Preference (%) for Novice Level

L1-PW group preferring L1 [9/14] for:

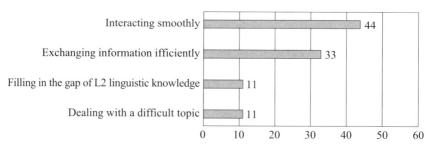

Figure 16. Reasons of L1 preference chosen by the novice level L1 pair-work group. There are four reasons listed on the left. The number of response is shown in square brackets as [the number of response divided by the total number of participants] above in the bar graph.

in other words, seemed to have influenced those participants who were willing to use the L2 for PW.

According to Figure 15, those participants who showed no preference of PW language provided various reasons, from which it is difficult to identify a certain consistency. The top three reasons, however, were identical to those of L2 preference (see Figure 14): practicing the language, using the same language as text and ST, and recalling text information efficiently.

According to Figure 16, the top three reasons to prefer the L1 use chosen by the novice level are related to the efficiency of communication (nearly 45%: interacting smoothly; 33%: exchanging information efficiently; 11%: filling in the gap of L2 linguistic knowledge). These results show that the participants with limited L2 skills have a desire to use the L1 for efficient communication. The other 11% showed L1 preference for the benefit of dealing with a difficult topic. Among

PRSQ (4): Survey Evaluation of PW Langauge Preference (%) for Novice Level

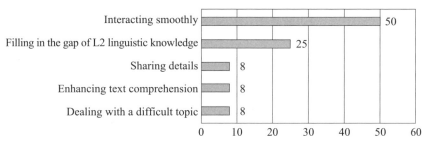

Figure 17. Reasons of L1 preference chosen by the novice level L2 pair-work group. There are five reasons listed on the left. The number of response is shown in square brackets as [the number of response divided by the total number of participants] above in the bar graph.

the same group, one participant showed L2 preference for the reason of practicing the language. Moreover, four participants showed no preference for the following four reasons: dealing with a difficult topic, using the same language as text and ST, practicing the language, and other reasons not on the list. These reasons were similar to the ones chosen by the upper-intermediate level L2-PW group for their L2 preference (see Figure 14), which seem related to metacognitive or metalinguistic awareness.

According to Figure 17, all the participants of L2-PW group for the novice level preferred the L1 for PW. Over two-thirds of the participants showed a desire to use the L1 for efficient communication (nearly 51%: interacting smoothly; 25%: filling in the gap of L2 linguistic knowledge). These results indicate, conversely, how much difficulty the novice participants faced during L2-PW.

5. Research Question (5): Language preference in different circumstances during a reading lesson

RQ (5) examined how the participants' language preference would vary depending on different circumstances during the reading lesson in general. The participants were asked to choose either the L1 or the L2 to use for the following eight circumstances: (a) when the teacher is explaining vocabulary, (b) when the teacher is explaining grammar rules and structure, (c) when the teacher isproviding answers to reading comprehension test (RCT), (d) when the teacher is explaining the answers of RCT, (e) when the teacher is asking students questions, (f) when the teacher is making classroom announcements, (g) when students are answering questions from the teacher, and (h) when students are having a discussion. The participants were asked these questions referring to the general L2 reading classroom (not limited to the conditions of the current

Table 9

Descriptive Statistics and Chi-square Test Summary Table for PRSQ (5): Language Preference x Circumstances in the Reading Lesson

	Teacher explaining vocabulary	Teacher explaining grammar & structures	Teacher providing answers to RCTs	Teacher explaining answers/ of RCT	Teacher asking questions	Teacher making classroom announcements	Students answering questions	Students having discussions
Prefer L1								
Count	55	83	37	79	33	87	39	54
% (count/total N)	53%	81%	36%	77%	32%	84%	38%	52%
Adjusted standardized residual	3.5	31.5	-14.5	27.5	-18.5	35.5	-12.5	2.5
Prefer L2								
Count	48	20	66	24	70	16	64	49
% (count/total N)	47%	19%	64%	23%	68%	16%	62%	48%
Adjusted standardized residual	-3.5	-31.5	14.5	-27.5	18.5	-35.5	12.5	-2.5
Total	103	103	103	103	103	103	103	103
Chi-square (χ^2)	.47	38.53	8.16	29.36	13.29	48.94	6.06	.24
df	1	1	1	1	1	1	1	1
p	.49	.00*	.00*	.00*	.00*	.00*	.01	.62
Cramer's V	.07	.61	.28	.53	.36	.69	.24	.05

Note: The alpha level for PRSQ (5) was adjusted to .000625 (.05 was divided by 8) according to Bonferroni's correction.
* $p < .05$

study). As explained previously, the purpose of PRSQ (5) was to examine general language use preference of Japanese university students. Therefore, the data obtained from the two cohorts, that is, upper-intermediate and novice levels, were combined and analyzed via a chi-square test regardless of their proficiency levels or experimental conditions. According to the results, the participants showed a significantly strong preference for the L1 to the L2 in the following three circumstances: when the teacher is explaining grammar rules and structure ($\chi^2[1$, N = 103] = 38.53, p =.00, Cramer's V = .61), when the teacher is explaining the answers of RCT ($\chi^2[1$, N = 103] = 29.36, p =.00, Cramer's V = .53), and when the teacher is making classroom announcements ($\chi^2[1$, N = 103] = 48.94, p =.00, Cramer's V = .69). In contrast, the same participants showed a significantly strong preference for the L2 to the L1 on the following two circumstances: when the teacher is providing answers to RCT ($\chi^2[1$, N = 103] = 8.16, p =.00, Cramer's V = .28) and the teacher is asking questions to students ($\chi^2[1$, N = 103] = 13.29, p =.00, Cramer's V = .36). These results are summarized in Table 9 on the previous page.

According to the results of RQs (1)–(5) described above, the essential findings of the current study can be summarized as follows.

1. Different language use during the pair work (PW) indicated little influence on reading comprehension, namely, results of summary completion test (ST) and delayed summary completion test (DST), for either the upper-intermediate level or the novice level. The types of tests (ST and DST), however, brought a significant influence on the L2-PW group within the novice level. That is, their scores on DST dropped considerably as compared to ST.

2. Different language use during PW influenced the PW production. The L1-PW groups for both upper-intermediate and novice levels outperformed the L2-PW groups significantly in terms of the scores of

Chapter III   The Study   99

PW focus questions.

3. The language used during PW influenced the results of numerical PW evaluation for the novice level. That is, the L1-PW group within the novice level evaluated PW significantly higher than the L2-PW group. In contrast, the upper-intermediate level did not show a significant difference between the L1 and L2 PW groups. As a general tendency of the current study, however, the vast majority of participants valued PW positively regardless of their PW language use or proficiency levels. Two common reasons for positive PW evaluation were "being able to understand the theme or main ideas" and "being able to share background knowledge." The difference between the two levels was that only the upper-intermediate level pointed out the reason "being able to understand details" for positive evaluation, whereas none of the novice level chose that reason.

4. Different language use during PW influenced the results of PW language preference (L1 preference, L2 preference, or no preference) for the upper-intermediate level. Within the upper-intermediate level, the ratio of PW language preference was significantly different between the L1 and L2 PW groups. On the other hand, the results for the novice level did not indicate such a difference. For the upper-intermediate level, the vast majority of L1-PW group preferred to use the L1. In contrast, the L2-PW group's preference split into three alternatives almost evenly. For the novice level, the majority of L1-PW group showed L1 preference, and the entire L2-PW group were in favor of the L1.

5. The participants' language preference varied according to different circumstances of the reading lesson. The participants preferred to use the L1 significantly more than the L2 when the teacher was explaining grammar rules or structures, explaining answers to reading

comprehension tests (RCTs), and making classroom announcements. In contrast, the same participants preferred to use the L2 when the teacher was providing answers to RCTs and asking questions.

With regard to the hypotheses, the following results can be addressed:

■ Hypothesis 1, which stated that L1 use during the peer interaction would facilitate cognitive processing and collaboration, resulting in better reading comprehension and memory retention compared to the case of L2 peer interaction, was not supported at a statistically significant level according to the results of RQ (1).

■ Hypothesis 2, which stated that L1 use during peer interaction in the form of pair work would facilitate interaction and enhance the quantity and quality of pair work outcomes; and also L1 pair work would be appreciated by students as compared to L2 pair work, was mostly supported by the results of RQ (2) and (3).

■ Hypothesis 3, which stated that language preference, in either the L1 or L2, would be influenced by students' L2 proficiency levels and circumstances of the lesson, was supported by the results of RQ (4) and (5).

The detailed discussion on the results above is presented in the next chapter.

Chapter IV

Discussion

A. Responses to Research Questions

The current study investigated whether the language use during the pair work (PW) would influence participants' reading comprehension and reading attitudes. Based on the results obtained, the researcher will respond to the five research questions (RQs) raised.

1. Research Question (1): Influence of language use on reading comprehension

The current study has found that there was no significant difference between the L1 and L2 PW groups in terms of participants' performance on the summary completion test (ST) or delayed summary completion test (DST) regardless of their language proficiency levels. In other words, the PW language use did not influence the participants' reading comprehension significantly as far as the results of current study showed. If the language use during PW makes little difference in terms of L2 reading comprehension, namely, the results of ST and DST, it seems possible for the teacher to choose either L1 or L2, taking into consideration students' proficiency level or the purpose of a lesson. For this decision making, the teacher also needs to consider the students' perception of language use, which will be discussed later in the discussion of Research Question (2).

Related to the results of Research Question (1), it is also worth considering that the L2-PW group of the novice level showed a significant drop from ST to DST scores. This could be interpreted to mean that the novice-level participants could not have efficiently stored the text information into long-term memory when they had the PW in the L2. As discussed in the Literature Review, students need to access their background knowledge in order to process newly obtained information and store it in their memory (Bransford, Brown & Cocking, 2000). For those novice-level participants, however, it seemed difficult to fully activate their background knowledge and share it with their partner via the L2 in order to construct a solid situation model in a collaborative manner. Kintsch (2009) pointed out that L2 reading itself is already cognitively demanding since the text information needs "to be translated to be understood" and little cognitive resource is left over for memory retention as a result (p.229). In consideration of these factors, the L2 PW at the novice level might not have been effective for refining a situation model collaboratively or for retaining memory.

In contrast, the L1-PW groups for both upper-intermediate and novice levels increased the scores from ST to DST, although not at a statistically significant level. This opposite result to the L2-PW groups could be explained by the fact that L1-PW groups had more active interaction in terms of quantity, that is, frequency of turn-taking, and quality, naemly results of PW focus questions, which played a role of anchoring the obtained text information. Kintsch (1983) explained memory as a "by-product of processing," and deeper or more elaborate processing tends to "leave more traces" in one's mind, which could be a trigger to retrieve certain information easily (p.335). This notion seems to support the benefit of L1-PW in terms of memory retention as well as lively interaction.

Chapter IV   Discussion   *103*

This interpretation, however, needs to be made while considering the fact that the difference between the L1 and L2 PW groups was not statistically significant. Therefore, further research is required based on extensive data, such as comparing L1, L2 and code-switching groups, before reaching a firm conclusion on this point. Nevertheless, it is hard to deny that L1-PW brought some positive influence on the participants accounting for (a) the L1-PW groups for both upper-intermediate and novice levels increased the scores from ST to DST; (b) the L1-PW groups for both levels surpassed the L2-PW groups in PW focus question scores significantly; and (c) L1-PW group within the novice level evaluated PW significantly higher than the L2-PW group. The last two points will be discussed in the following sections, research questions (2) and (3) accordingly, more in detail.

2. Research Question (2): Influence of language use on the outcomes of pair work

The L1-PW groups for both upper-intermediate and novice levels obtained significantly higher scores on PW focus questions. Hence, it is clear that L1 use during PW enhanced the PW production and its accuracy. There seems to be two possible ways to explain the result. One is that the L1-PW groups were able to exchange more information freely and to have more opportunities to negotiate meaning during PW. Consequently, they were able to refine their "situation model" (or mental representations) of the reading text collaboratively. The researcher does not mean to simply imply that L1 use guarantees successful collaboration or active interaction, since those outcomes require well-planned preparatory activities, such as checking comprehension of a given task or sharing background information and strategies needed for a pair work. However, L1 use will be some help if the problem only lies in students'

104

English proficiency, which prevents them from conducting adequate pair work. The other possible factor to explain why L1 use brought positive effects on PW production is that the L1-PW groups had no linguistic burden in producing written responses to PW focus questions compared to the L2-PW groups. This echoes with the study results by Sweetnam Evants (2011: see Advantages of L1 use by students in Chapter II). Moreover, in relation to Cummins' Quadrants described in Literature Review, the majority of the participants seemed to have few contextual clues since they were not familiar with the subsequent topic (anorexia), as revealed by the results of the buffer task gauging the amount of their background knowledge on the topic. In terms of cognitive load, on the other hand, the L2-PW groups, especially at the novice level, must have had a cognitively heavy load due to L2 use during pair work; whereas the L1-PW groups seemed to have had comparatively less cognitive load since the language tools to discuss the focus questions were fully automatized. In other words, under the conditions of the current study, L1 PW can be categorized as a task belonging to quadrant C, whereas L2 PW can be identified as a quadrant-D task (see Figure 4).

The positive influence of the L1 use on the outcomes of pair work discussed above can be supported by some extracts of audio-recorded PW as well. That is, the frequency of turn-taking within the L1 pairs exceeded that of the L2 pairs regardless of their proficiency levels. The results analyzed by a t-test are summarized in Table 10 on the following page.

Although the difference between the groups for each level was not statistically significant, the effect size was large for both levels, which means the L1 and L2 PW groups at each level were quite different regarding the frequency of turn-taking. In other words, more turn-takings occurred within the L1-pairs during PW under the condition of the current

Table 10

Descriptive Statistics and t-test Summary Tables on Turn-taking during PW

Descriptive Statistics and t-test Summary Tables on Turn-taking during PW for Upper-intermediate Level

PW	Mean	SD	t	df	p	Effect size (Cohen's d)
L1-PW (n = 4)	142.50	33.32	–	–	–	–
L2-PW (n = 4)	113.50	32.94	–	–	–	–
Total	128.00	33.13	1.23	6	.26	.88

Note: "n" represents the number of pairs. The participants' number was 8 for each PW group.

Descriptive Statistics and t-test Summary Tables on Turn-taking during PW

Descriptive Statistics and t-test Summary Tables on Turn-taking during PW for Novice Level

PW	Mean	SD	t	df	p	Effect size (Cohen's d)
L1-PW (n = 4)	102.00	41.46	–	–	–	–
L2-PW (n = 4)	60.25	22.27	–	–	–	–
Total	81.12	31.86	1.77	6	.12	1.26

Note: "n" represents the number of pairs. The participants' number was 8 for each PW group.

study. Especially for the novice level, the L1-PW pairs took over 1.5 times more turns than their counterparts.

Not only the quantity of peer interaction but also its quality seems to be influenced by PW language use as well as by the proficiency levels. In order to support this argument, the researcher will show the following four extracts from the recorded PW. To facilitate the comparison, all extracts were chosen for the same question, PW focus question (2):

How people's perspectives on anorexia have changed for the last ten years? Regarding all the extracts, the L1 interaction was translated by the researcher, which was attached in square brackets. Within the L2 interaction, the L2 words with foreign pronunciations and the inserted L1 words or expressions were italicized, with their translations attached in square brackets. L2 grammar mistakes were underlined. Each participant was indicated by his or her initials.

First, the researcher will introduce two extracts from the upper-intermediate level pairs. The upper-intermediate level, in general, was able to negotiate meanings in order to construct situation models collaboratively, not only via the L1 but also via the L2. The upper-intermediate level seemed to be capable of sharing and confirming the text information constructively, rephrasing difficult L2 words or expressions, and maintaining peer interaction without facing communication breakdown. Through the process of such active peer interaction, they were able to figure out the answers for the focus questions. The following Extract 1 shows the interaction of an L1 pair and Extract 2 shows the interaction of an L2 pair.

Extract 1: An upper-intermediate level L1 pair discussing PW focus question (2)

1 TY   Kore sakki kaitayo-ne? Ju-nen mae wa karada-no byoki.
        [We wrote this for the previous question, didn't we? It was considered as a physical problem 10 years ago.]

2 YR   Karada-ni henka-ga arawareru-toka.
        [There was like a physical change.]

3 TY   Taberare-nai-tte-iu karada-no byoki dato omotte ita. Sore-ga ima-wa kokoro-kara kuru byoki?
        [I thought it was a physical disease that a patient could not

eat. But now it is considered as a mental disease?]

4 YR   Un so dane.

        [Yes, that's right.]

5 TY   Somo-somo byoki dato omoware-te ita no kana?

        [Was it considered as a disease at the beginning?]

6 YR   Dou nan-da ro?

        [I am not sure.]

7 TY   Ima-wa byoki toshite nin-tei sareta-kedo.

        [It is approved as a disease now.]

8 YR   Mukashi-wa tada ijo mitai-na, nan-ka son-na-koto kaite-atta
        yone? Watashi-ga tada tekito-ni itte-nai yone?

        [The text said that it was considered simply as an unusual
        condition in the past, didn't it? Am I just imagining that?]

9 TY   To-omou. Nan-daka daietto no i-sshu mitaina.

        [I think so too. It was something like an diet.]

10 YR   Kaite atta-ne.

        [Yes, it was written in the text.]

Extract 1 (upper-intermediate level, L1 pair) indicates that both participants contributed to the interaction equally by sharing the information. For instance, one of the participant started a sentence and the partner finished it (turns 7–8). They also raised a question to confirm the information collaboratively (turns 8–10).

Extract 2: The upper-intermediate level L2 pair discussing PW focus question (2)

1 HM   Can you recall --- (reading the question)? Ah, anorexia.

2 MS   I think ten years ago, anorexia don't, doesn't, isn't so
        important, but today it is danger.

3 HM   Umm.

4	MS	Some people die because of this. I don't remember it is in this edi---, editorial, but today is difficult and dangerous problem. I think.
5	HM	Why, why did you think ten years ago, umm, the anorexia is not important?
6	MS	I cannot remember, but I think it is written in the editorial, and --- umm, I cannot remember the exact words. Umm--- I cannot give, some, more information.
7	HM	Umm. And what mean the "perspective?"
8	MS	This mean view. People see the anorexia important or not important.
9	HM	Ah, OK, OK.
10	MS	How people think about anorexia?
11	HM	I think so and ---
12	MS	But the reason is ---
13	HM	Umm. Why not important? Umm--- ah--- Now we, *Etto* [well], Physical, ahh---
14	MS	Physical what?
15	HM	Physical problem is very, very --- Many people have physical problem, but ten years ago, ahh---, umm---.
16	MS	Umm---. Physical? Not mental?
17	HM	Mental, mental, yes. *Sou-sou* [That's right]. Mental --- (time was up).
		Ah, I didn't tell you.

Extract 2 (upper-intermediate level, L2 pair) shows that the pair managed to discuss the question without facing a serious communication breakdown. Both participants contributed to the interaction almost evenly. They were able to ask questions and provide information to each other, for instance, turns 1–2. Their L2 level was high enough to do self-correction, such as correcting a verb form: turn 2, clarify the meaning of unknown word ("perspective": turns 7–9), and correct the other one's utterance ("physical" → "mental": turns 16–17). It took, however, too much time to get to the point of discussion. Although the upper-intermediate seemed linguistically capable to conduct L2 PW, they ended up running out of time (turn 17).

Next, the researcher will introduce three extracts from novice-level pairs. For the novice level, in general, the L1 use helped the participants to interact smoothly. Due to the lack of detailed information, however, they sometimes relied on "guessing" too much. As Coté et al. (1998) noted, this is a typical example of "assimilated reading," where readers use background knowledge and they make guesses excessively in order to compromise lack of solid textbase. This sometimes brings a positive result, but other times the result is negative. Such an example can be observed in Extract 3 below, where the novice participants were having L1-PW.

Extract 3: The novice level L1 pair discussing PW focus question (2)

1 MR   Gen-in-ga wakan-nai-tte iu hanashi ja-nai? Gen-zai dewa ---
        [Isn't this a story that they don't know the reason? Now ---]

2 TT   Kyo-shoku-sho kanja ga gen-zai dewa---
        [Now anorexia patients ---]

3 MR   Sou-sou. Genzai-dewa seishin-teki-na mono-ga genin-to
        iuno-ga wakatta mitai-na.
        [That's right. Now we know the cause is related to mental
        problem. Something like that.]

4 TT   Seishin-teki-na mondai ---
        [Mental problem ---]

5 MR   ---tte-koto-ga wakatta. Ja ju-nen-mae wa wakanna-katta-tte

koto-kana?

Gyaku-o ie-ba ju-nen-mae wa wakanna-katta-tte koto-kana?

[Yes, that was revealed. Then, they did not know it ten years ago. Does it imply that they did not know it ten years ago?]

6 TT Naa. Yayakoshii byoki-tte iuno-wa wakatte-tanja nai-no?

[They knew that it was a complicated problem, didn't they?]

7 MR Un. Ja yayakoshii byoki-tte iuno-o kakeba? Ju-nen-mae no tokoro-ni.

De kocchi-ga nan-de yayakoshii-ka-tte itta-ra seishin-ga kakawatte-iru-kara.

[Yes. So why don't you write it in the section of "ten years ago?" And then, why was it a complicated problem? Because it was related to one's mental condition.]

8 TT Himan-kara dakkyaku-suru tame-ni toka-wa nakatta-kke?

[Wasn't there a part talking about treatingdiabetes?]

9 MR Atta. Sono himan-kara dakkyaku-suru tame-ni muri-na shokuji-seigen-o shitakara nante-no taicho kuzushi-te kyoshoku-sho-ni natte sukkari otoroe-te-shimatta.

[Yes, there was. In order to treat diabetes, they went on too much of a diet, and, what shall I say, they became anorexic, which ruined their health and made them completely weak.]

Extract 3 (novice level, L1-pair) shows that both participants contributed to the interaction equally. They were able to make a logical guess based on the text information (turn 5: If it [anorexia] is now known as a mental problem, its cause must have been unknown in the past). The same participants, however, made a wrong guess (turn 9: The cause of anorexia is an excessive diet in order to treat diabetes). They assumed that the relationship between diabetes and anorexia was one of "cause and effect," which was not supported by the text information. In this case, therefore, their guessing went too far probably due to the lack of detailed information elicited from the text. Although they did not succeed in constructing a correct situation model on this point, they were at least able to maintain the interaction, negotiate meanings, and reach a conclusion. In that sense, they conducted and completed the task "successfully" in their own way. This is the important first step, the researcher believes, for the class participation and positive self-evaluation. By going through this step, the novice students would be encouraged to play a more active role during the lesson, which will promote their L2 learning.

In contrast, the novice level L2-pairs had hardly any meaning negotiation during PW. In most cases, it took them too long to figure out the meaning of the question. They simply listed keywords, but could not articulate any sentence to share or ask for necessary information. Consequently, they kept silent and ran out of time, or ended up using the L1 with a sense of guilt and failure. It is ironic that the more seriously participants tried to follow the L2 use rule, the fewer opportunities they had for productive peer interaction. The following Extract 4 shows an example of communication breakdown, while Extract 5 shows a case where participants failed to figure out the meaning of the question.

Extract 4: The novice level L2 pair (#1) discussing PW focus question (2)

1 KK Umm--- (long silence)
2 AC Umm --- (long silence), *ano-rexi-sar* [anorexia] is --- umm --- not famous. *Byo-jo ja nakatta* [it was not a symptom]. More famous than fat.
3 KK Not famous --- (long silence).
4 AC *Chigau ki-ga suru-kedo* [I don't think it is correct].

This pair took turns only four times within four minutes, and the rest of the conversation was filled with long periods of silence. The utterances were very short, probably due to the fact that they tried to follow the L2-only rule. They had code-switching twice in turns 2 and 4. In turn 2, the student intended to say that "the anorexia was not a well-known symptom," but she misused the word "famous," which seemed to have confused her partner. In turn 4, the same student used the L1 even for a simple L2 sentence, "I don't think it is correct." It seems likely that this code-switching occurred due to her lack of confidence in L2 PW. During their L2 PW, they were not able to articulate any L2 sentence. As a result, they hardly had meaningful interaction. In addition, it was painful for the researcher to listen to the recording due to the long and uncomfortable silence. It can be easily assumed that the actual participants of PW must have had a similar feeling. This is one of the results of compelling a novice to use only the L2 during a lesson.

Extract 5: The novice level L2-pair (#2) discussing PW focus question (2)

1	SS	I don't know. I don't know.
2	MY	Oh, no. *A chotto* [Oh, wait].
3	SS	I don't know this word.
4	MY	What do you mean *E-di-to-ri* ---
5	SS	Mou [Well], I don't know.
6	MY	*Kyoshoku-sho* [Anorexia]. Can you recall --- yes or no?
7	SS	*Iiya chigau chigau* [No, no it is not].
8	MY	Yes or no problem?
9	SS	*Chigau-yaro* [It is not, I guess].
10	MY	*Oshiete-kuda-sai* [Tell me]. Teach me!
11	SS	Can you recall --- means?

12	MY	Teach me --- *mitaina* [something like that].
13	SS	*Ee?* [Really?]
14	MY	This person? *Kyoshoku-sho* [Anorexia].
15	SS	*Su-pe-ru-ga waka-ran* [I don't know the spelling].
16	MY	*A-no-rex* --- in the hospital.

Extract 5 shows the interaction of another novice L2-pair struggling to figure out the meaning of the question. Although they code-switched many times (turns 2, 5–7, 9–10, 12–16), they failed to grasp the meaning of the question. During the interaction, they never got to the content discussion and they expressed their frustration constantly (turns 2, 5, 10, 15). If they had had a chance to discuss the meaning of focus questions in the L1 as a preparatory activity, they might have been able to take part in more productive L2 interaction. Moreover, with some knowledge of simple classroom English, such as "please wait," "tell me," or "I don't know the spelling," they could have engaged in L2 PW with less stress.

To summarize the discussion on RQ (2) above, PW language use seems to influence PW production. Indeed, the L1-PW enhanced PW production significantly. The advantage of L1-PW mainly stems from the following two factors: (a) the L1-pairs were able to exchange information as well as negotiate meaning freely without facing any linguistic difficulties; and (b) the L1-pairs were able to express what they had discussed during PW as written responses without worrying about L2 grammar rules or expressions. Therefore, it can be said that the L1 is a valuable tool if the purpose of an activity is to have active interaction in order to better comprehend the text or topic. Especially at the novice level, where participation tends to be limited under the L2 only environment, L1-PW would provide students with more opportunities and confidence to contribute to the lesson.

In addition, the recorded PW revealed an affective factor influenced by L1 use during PW. That is, the participants of L1-PW for both levels seem to have felt satisfaction and confidence. More precisely, the L1-pairs produced several utterances of positive self-evaluation, such as "We were able to write quite a lot"; "We did pretty well on this question"; or "We did a god job." In contrast, none of the L2-pair produced such comments during PW. Although such affective factors are not usually measured by a numerical comprehension test, most teachers know that a positive atmosphere for pair- or class-work is crucial for learning. If L1 use opens up more opportunities for students, i.e., especially at the novice level, to participate in the lesson actively with a sense of satisfaction and confidence, the teacher should not hesitate to use the L1 in order to create a better learning environment.

These positive outcomes of the L1 PW especially at the novice level were reflected in the results of PRSQ (1) (numerical PW evaluation), where the L1-PW group at the novice level valued PW significantly higher than the L2-PW group, as discussed below.

3. Research Question (3): Influence of language use on pair-work evaluation

The language use during PW influenced the results of numerical PW evaluation of the novice level. That is, the L1-PW group valued PW significantly higher than the L2-PW group. On the other hand, the upper-intermediate level did not indicate any difference between the L1and L2 PW groups. These results suggest that the novice participants, whose linguistic skills are limited, tend to appreciate L1 use during PW more than the upper-intermediate level, who are capable of conducting PW in either language if necessary. The results within the novice level were similar to the ones of previous research (Matsumoto, 2013), where L1 and L2 pre-reading activities were examined within the intermediate level and the L1 group appreciated the pre-reading activities significantly more than the L2 group with regard to the summary writing task. These findings from the current study and the previous research seem to indicate that L1 use in peer-interaction tends to be appreciated by the participants mainly due to the benefits for smooth communication and enhanced reading comprehension, such as understanding the theme or main ideas.

As a general tendency of the current study, however, the vast majority of participants valued PW positively regardless of their PW language use or proficiency levels. These results support the importance of peer interaction for reading comprehension described in the Literature Review.

The survey showed that two common reasons among all participants for positive PW evaluation were "being able to understand the theme or main ideas" and "being able to share background knowledge." These are crucial factors for enhancing reading comprehension. As explained in the Literature Review section (see Mechanism of reading), the essential information elicited from the text, such as the theme or main ideas, needs to be synthesized with readers' background knowledge in order to comprehend the text. If the participants realized that PW was useful for such process, the peer interaction must have played a significant role for their reading.

On the other hand, there were noticeable differences between the upper-intermediate and novice levels. The first difference concerned whether the participants were able to share details during PW or not. In fact, only the upper-intermediate level participants indicated this reason for their positive PW evaluation, while none of the novice level participants pointed it out. This difference apparently came from their language proficiency levels. In order to elicit detailed information from the text, a certain level of L2 proficiency is required. Therefore, the novice participants might not have found any benefit of PW for this reason. Even if they had some detailed information elicited from the text, their limited L2 skills would have prevented them from sharing it with their partner in the case of L2-PW.

The other difference between the two levels was that one-third of novice level participants appreciated PW for "being able to share background knowledge," whereas only 7% of the upper-intermediates cited the same reason. This gap between the two levels seems to imply that the novice participants tried to utilize their background knowledge in order to compensate for the lack of detailed information. This type of reading is described by Coté, Goldman and Saul (1998) as "assimilated mental representation," where readers heavily rely on their prior knowledge in order to make up for poorly constructed textbase. The combination of poorly constructed textbase and too much reliance on one's prior knowledge might bring either a positive or negative result. The teacher, therefore, needs to show students how to construct more solid textbase as well as to guide them for more logical guessing.

To summarize the significant findings regarding RQ (3), the following four points can be pointed out. First, the L1-PW was appreciated significantly more than the L2-PW at the novice level. Second, both the upper-intermediate and novice levels evaluated PW positively for the reasons of being able to understand the theme or main ideas and being able to share background knowledge. Third, only the upper-intermediate level participants chose the reason of being able to share details for their positive PW evaluation, which suggests that the novice participants were not able to share enough details during PW mainly due to their limited L2 decoding skills or L2 communication skills. Fourth, one-third of the novice participants chose the reason of being able to share background knowledge for their positive PW evaluation, which could indicate that some novice participants needed to rely on the background knowledge to fill in the gap of missing details.

Based on these findings, the researcher will raise the following two points, focusing on the novice level students. First, it appears to be more effective for novice students to have some support in decoding the reading text in order to construct firm textbase. For instance, the teacher can provide several focus questions to students for eliciting main ideas or necessary details in order to guide their reading comprehension. Second, students should also be provided enough opportunities to share their background knowledge freely with others so that they can fill in missing pieces of the individual situation model. The teacher needs to observe their peer interaction and offer some directions if they stray from constructing coherent textbase or situation models. Such peer interaction seems to be beneficial not only for helping reading comprehension but also for boosting students' participation and confidence. For these two purposes, the L1 plays a fundamental role. If the focus is to enhance reading comprehension, not to practice language use, the L1 seems more suitable for the novice level. In fact, these two goals, namely, enhancing reading comprehension and practicing L2 use, should be considered separately, at least for certain proficiency levels. The researcher will discuss this point further in the Pedagogical Implications section.

4. Research Question (4): Influence of language use on language preference for pair work

Language use during PW influenced PW language preference at the upper-intermediate level, while the novice level's PW language preference was not significantly influenced by the actual language use during PW. In the following section, the researcher will examine the results of each level accordingly.

■ Upper-intermediate level

Language use during PW had a significant influence on PW language preference at the upper-intermediate level. In other words, the ratio of the participants' language preference (L1 preference, L2 preference, or no preference) was markedly different between the L1 and L2 PW groups. The vast majority of L1-PW group (87%) showed an L1 preference. In contrast, the responses of L2-PW group almost evenly split among the three alternatives. These results suggest that the upper-intermediate level was capable of conducting PW via the L2 when they were encouraged to do so. With consideration to the fact that nearly half of the L2-PW group either preferred using the L2 (23%) or did not mind using the L2 (i.e., no preference: 36%) for PW, it can be said that they did not show a negative reaction against L2 use during PW as the novice level participants did, as will be discussed later. At the same time, the L1-PW group clearly recognized the value of L1 use during PW. Therefore, it seems possible for the teacher to choose either the L1 or L2 during PW at the upper-intermediate level, depending on the purpose of the lesson.

The survey evaluation of PW language preference indicated that the L1 was preferred mainly for the efficiency of interaction and for enhancing the depth of reading. In contrast, the L2 was preferred for reasons related to metalinguistic or metacognitive awareness, such as using the same language as text and summary completion test, practicing the language, or recalling text information efficiently. In other words, the L1 was chosen according to the participants' natural desire for having efficient interaction and better comprehension, whereas, the L2 was chosen intentionally based on participant's metalinguistic or metacognitive awareness.

■Novice level

There was no significant difference between the groups within the novice level. The majority of L1-PW group (64%) preferred using the L1 for PW mainly for the reason of efficient interaction. This seems natural considering the results of numerical evaluation of PW and PW production, both of which were significantly positive for the L1-PW group. Obviously the L1-PW group benefitted from the L1 use for the PW production and appreciated it. In contrast, the L2-PW group showed a marked negative reaction to L2 use. That is, 100% of them preferred to use the L1 for PW. From this result, it is clear that the L2-PW group had considerable difficulty in conducting PW via the L2. They were in favor of the L1 largely for the efficiency of interaction, which is same as for the L1-PW group.

To summarize the results obtained from the novice level, L2 use during PW was too much of a burden for them, and they were willing to use the L1 for the sake of efficient interaction. Considering their limited L2 language skills, it makes more sense to use the L1 during PW in order to have active interaction, such as sharing information and negotiating meaning. Through this process, it seems possible for students to refine the individually constructed situation model of the text. Such collaboration is especially needed for the weak L2 readers. If we assume that the purpose of PW is to help those readers enhance their reading comprehension, the focus should be on the quality and quantity of interaction, not the language they use during PW. Therefore, it is necessary for the teacher to reconsider the purpose of PW before enforcing novice-level students to use the L2, which might end up depriving students of valuable opportunities for information exchange and negotiation of meaning.

5. Research Question (5): Language preference in different circumstances during a reading lesson

The current study revealed participants' distinctive preference of language use depending on different circumstances of a L2 reading lesson. That is, the L1 was preferred when the teacher clarifies grammar rules and structures, explains answers of reading comprehension tests (RCTs), and makes classroom announcements; whereas the L2 was preferred when the teacher provides answers to RCTs and asks students questions. As discussed previously, the L1 seems to be preferred when students want to understand the content of the teacher's output, whereas the L2 appears to be preferred when students can expect certain linguistic patterns of interaction, which they might consider as opportunities to practice receiving L2 input. In addition, though it was not at a statistically significant level, the majority of participants (62%) was in favor of the L2 for answering questions asked by the teacher. This seems to indicate that the participants would be willing to produce L2 output with the help of appropriately provided linguistic tools or background knowledge. In order to set up such conditions, the L1 can be utilized for the novice level in particular.

6. Summary

As discussed above in response to research questions (2) and (3), the results of current study have shown some positive influences of L1 use with regard to students' PW production and PW evaluation. Although the direct influence of language use on reading comprehension as has been examined in the form of RQ (1) was not identified at a statistically significant level, the noticeable score drop from the summary completion test to the delayed summary completion test indicated a possible difficulty for the novice-level participants to use the L2 for effective interaction and memory retention. These findings seem to be related to Cummins' idea of "common underlying proficiency" (2001) discussed in the Literature Review section. In order to conduct effective peer interaction, it is crucial to make use of students' cognitive resources that lie underneath the surface features of their L1 or L2, such as background knowledge on a given topic or skills to make logical inferences. Toward that end, students need to access and share cognitive resources with other students. When students' L2 language skills are limited, their L1 will be a useful tool to facilitate interaction, possibly resulting in enhanced L2 learning and also raising the level of students' participation and motivation.

Research question (4) found that the novice-level participants strongly preferred the L1 use for PW, while the upper-intermediate level seemed to be able to use either L1 or L2 for PW. This finding indicates that the L2 proficiency level needs to be considered in choosing the appropriate PW language. In addition, different circumstances of a lesson are also crucial factors to consider for deciding language use. According to Research Question (5), the L1 was preferred by the participants to understand precisely the content of the given information, while the L2 was preferred when certain linguistic patterns of interaction that are considered as opportunities to practice L2 interaction could be expected. These findings seem to echo Littlewood's twofold focus of L2 learning and teaching (2004), which are analytical activities and experiential activities. The analytical activities can be aimed at understanding content either about a language or a given topic. In contrast, the experiential activities can be described as opportunities to be exposed to L2 use. Therefore, it can be said that the participants of the current study instinctively chose the L1 for analytical activities and the L2 for experiential activities, accordingly.

The results of the current study will provide the teacher with some hints to decide how and when to use the L1 or L2 during a lesson. In other words, the issues of language use during the lesson should not be discussed in an "all or nothing" manner. There seems to be certain circumstances where the L1 or L2 is preferred even within a lesson. In this sense, too, the exclusive L2 use or elimination of the L1 does not seem suitable for the L2 classroom. It is important for the individual teacher to figure out appropriate circumstances of L1 and L2 use during the lesson flexibly, based on students' level, the settings and purposes of a specific task, and the goals of a lesson. Moreover, any teaching guidelines or related research should help teachers to make the right decision by providing practical suggestions based on empirical research, instead of forcing them to use a specific language or method without considering the particular conditions.

In order to make a definitive statement about the influences of language use during PW, further research is obviously needed; however, the findings of the current study seem to open up an opportunity to consider a flexible way to utilize the L1 for L2 learning.

B. Pedagogical Implications

A purpose of the current study has been to present effective ways to use the L1 as a support of L2 learning. Based on the literature review and the results of the current study, the researcher now suggests the following three models with different focuses: (a) language use and a twofold focus on L2 learning and teaching, (b) language use in the process of L2 lessons, and (c) language use adapted for the students' proficiency level and the circumstances of the lesson.

1. Language use and a twofold focus of L2 learning and teaching

As discussed in Chapter I, communicative language teaching (CLT) has been a dominant teaching approach in many countries, and also it has been promoted in Japan. Therefore, the researcher will discuss the twofold focus of L2 learning and teaching under the framework of CLT.

There seems to be several factors which CLT has stemmed from. According to Howatt (2004), the realization emerged at the end of the 1960s that "language was not just a set of structure-habits, nor a collection of situationally sensitive phrases" (p.337), and this emerging view pushed forward the pedagogical movement of "relating form and meaning in the real world of language use" (p.326). At the same time, it was also realized that common notions are expressed in different languages, and they could be primary targets of language teaching programs. As a result, more studies on related topics were developed, such as analyzing communicative needs or identifying "common core," which is the minimum requirement for language learners to become independent language users and to move on to learn more specialized subjects. In relation to "common core," the notional/functional approach has been developed, which focuses on both linguistic knowledge and communicative function (Wilkins, 1976; van Ek, 1875/1980; as cited in Howatt, 2004, p.339). Since the notional/functional approach is considered to share much in common with CLT, it seems natural that the twofold focus of L2 learning and teaching proposed by Littlewood (2004), that is, analytical activities and experiential activities, can be synthesized under the frame of CLT.

CLT is roughly divided into two categories. One is the strong version, which encourages students to learn the target language (TL) exclusively through TL communication. This version, therefore, tends to avoid explicit form-focused instruction. The other is the weak version of CLT, which does not exclude instruction on grammar and form for the purpose of having TL communication. The L1 use tends to be discouraged in both versions. Given the EFL environment, where the opportunities for students to receive L2 input or to produce L2 output are limited, however, it seems extremely difficult to learn TL rules and expressions inductively without any form-focused instruction. Moreover, as Brown (2000) pointed out, those NNS teachers who have limited TL proficiency will face difficulties in conducting an effective lesson since CLT requires the teacher to create a learning environment where students use the TL "productively and receptively, in unrehearsed context" (p.267). In addition to such problems, Littlewood (2014) also noted difficulties in implementing CLT in Asia (EFL environment) not only in terms of instruction or classroom management via English but also because the respective goals of CLT and L2 instruction for traditional entrance examinations are contradictory. Littlewood, therefore, suggested that the strong and weak versions of CLT should be combined and adapted for the unique EFL environment. He called this "communication-oriented language teaching (COLT)," and COLT has stressed for the importance of including both "analytical and experiential" activities in the lesson (p.357). The continuum of two elements (Littlewood, 2004, p.322) are illustrated in Figure 18 on the following page, in which the language use and the interaction of each activity are also indicated by arrows (added by the researcher).

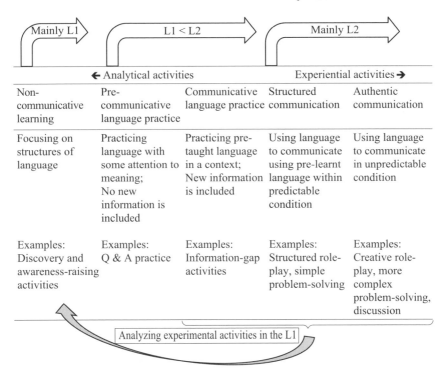

Figure 18. Continuum from analytical activities to experiential activities. Adapted from "The task-based approach: Some questions and suggestions" by W. Littlewood, 2004, *ELT Journal, 58*, p.322. Copyright 2004 by Oxford University Press. Adapted with permission.

Note: The figure indicates five categories of L2 communicative activities, to which the researcher added the amount of L1 and L2 use in each situation and the interaction between analytical and experiential activities.

As Figure 18 indicates, students can go through each activity from left to right in a step-by-step manner so that they can cover both focuses of L2 instruction. Although it seems less stressful for the novice students to start from analytical activities and proceed to experiential activities, the order of the two activities could be reversed as well. That is, a lesson could begin with experimental activities, so that students can realize what they are missing for communication in context, and then they can move to analytical activities such as learning about necessary expressions and practicing how to use them. The essential point of this model is that two types of activities are effectively combined and circulated throughout the lesson. L1 use can provide useful support toward that end. Regarding language use, Littlewood suggested that the L1 can be used, accordingly, at the following three stages:

- the presentation stage (Non-communicative learning) for enhancing the efficiency of instruction and communication as well as for accelerating students' progress,

- the practice stage ([Pre-]communicative language practice) uses the L1 for facilitating students' L2 use, and

- the production stage (Structured and Authentic communication) uses the L1 is for setting up a meaningful context of L2 communication (2014, p.359).

As students become more advanced, it is natural that the L1 use described above in each stage can be replaced by the L2 use.

The researcher strongly supports this Littlewood's notion of the twofold focus of L2 learning and teaching (i.e., facilitating analytical and experiential activities) with five-category framework as well as his suggestion for L1 use at each stage. In order to make the learning process more efficient under the EFL environment, rather explicit form-focused instruction through the analytical activities will be beneficial for students, which will enable them to learn the target language more or less deductively. By using the L1 during the analytical activities, students can concentrate on exploring the analysis or discussion itself without worrying about L2 production. Indeed, the participants in the current study preferred the L1 as a pair work language for interacting smoothly and sharing details (see the results of PRSQ [4]: Figures 12, 13, 16, and 17). Moreover, such analytical activities can be expanded to sharing background knowledge

Chapter IV   Discussion   *127*

or to discussing a given topic as pre-reading or post-reading activities. In fact, the results of current study have revealed that L1 use during the pair work enhances quantity and quality of pair-work production significantly (see the results of RQ [2]). Since the pair work of the current study required the participants to analyze and discuss the text according to the focus questions, it can be said that their L1 use facilitated the analytical activities. In addition, as discussed in the section of Pedagogical support for L1 use in the Literature Review, teachers' L1 use enhances the efficiency and accuracy of L2 instruction, which appears to set up a firm basis for analytical activities. Consequently, these arguments suggest that the optimal L1 use is beneficial for analytical activities, where students can learn about the L2 materials, including language and content, in a meta cognitive way. According to Cummins' idea of common underlying proficiency (2001), as described in the Literature Review, students have cognitive resources underneath the surface features of their L1 or L2. In order to make use of these variable resources for L2 learning, the L1 could be a trigger to elicit necessary information.

On the other hand, L2 use should be strongly encouraged during the experiential activities. As reviewed in the Peer Interaction section, actual L2 use through the interaction (i.e., experiential activities) will provide students with valuable opportunities for noticing a problem, paying attention to a specific form or expression, negotiating meaning, and enhancing the control over L2 use. These activities are not limited to oral interaction; they also include reporting the results of pair or group discussion to the class or summarizing reading texts and one's own opinions in a written form. Bearing in mind the importance of L2 experiential activities, how is it possible, then, to maximize the opportunities for students to use the L2 during the lesson? One way to attain this goal is for teachers to use the L1 effectively. This may sound contradictory, but as discussed in the Literature Review chapter, the L1 can be used for giving concise instruction, explaining the purpose of the activity, and having students well-equipped with necessary language tools. Such preparation will enable students to participate in L2 experiential activities with sense of security and motivation. As Butzkamm (2003) noted, the L1 plays a significant role to establish "the target language as the main medium of communication" (p. 32). At the same time, meaningful L2 experiential activities will lead students to discover important topics for analytical activities either about language use or the content of interaction as discussed above. This dynamic circulation between analytical and experiential activities (see Figure 18) seems crucial for L2 learning, especially in an EFL environment.

Moreover, the twofold focus of L2 instruction described above seems to echo the notion of "external and internal goals of learning" presented by V. Cook (2002). According to his definition, the external goals of language learning are related to the actual L2 use (mainly in oral communication) for practical purposes, such as shopping, traveling, or business negotiation. On the other hand, the internal goals of language learning focus on cultivating one's own mind for better cultural understanding or for more flexible thinking (p.330). Although the internal learning does not seem to contribute to L2 production directly as a tool, it is crucial as a fundamental cognitive source for meaningful communication. V. Cook pointed out that current English classrooms tend to mainly emphasize the external goals and to pay little attention to the internal goals, despite the fact that both goals of language learning are equally important (pp.330–331). Indeed what students need to develop for the global setting of English (L2) communication is not only L2 language skills but also the meaningful content to convey, as discussed in the Literature Review (Theoretical Support for L1 Use). If analytical activities, such as metacognitive and metalinguistic discussion, as well as content-focused discussion via the L1, can lead students more toward the internal goals of learning, they should be promoted by all means.

To summarize, it is more efficient for EFL classes to include both analytical and experiential activities optimally as a crucial twofold focus of L2 learning and teaching. These two focal points could also be linked to internal and external goals of learning. The language use for each focus can be roughly categorized as the L1 for analytical activities and the L2 for experiential activities, though the amount of L1 and L2 use needs to be flexible in accordance with students' proficiency level and lesson content.

2. Language use in the process of L2 lesson

One of the difficulties of L2 instruction via the L2 lies in the fact that the L2 becomes not only the object of learning but also the tool for learning. Especially when students are not advanced enough to use the "tool" freely, their learning itself tends to be hindered, which is a vicious cycle. In order to avoid such a frustrating situation, the researcher suggests the following pedagogical code-switching at least for the introductory stage. That is, mainly the L1 can be used for learning about the language or background knowledge about a given topic, while the L2 use is encouraged during, what Littlewood (2014) calls, "experiential activities," where students can learn how the language works in a meaningful context. Although this dichotomy should be treated flexibly, depending on students' proficiency levels or the purpose of a lesson, it could be one of the guidelines for language choice in the L2 classroom. In addition, this pedagogical code-switching will help students to realize the focus of each activity once they come to understand the reasons for language choice. As an example, the researcher will summarize the language use in a reading

130

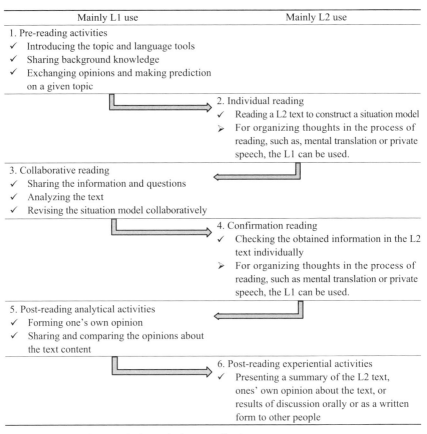

Figure 19. Sample L1 and L2 use during a reading lesson.

lesson in Figure 19 above.

As Figure 19 shows, the L1 and L2 are interwoven at each stage of the lesson. Following the previously discussed framework of the twofold focus for L2 learning and teaching (Littlewood, 2004), the L1 activities listed in the left column can be categorized as analytical activities, while L2 activities listed in the right column are categorized as experiential activities. A successful example of using two languages along with the lesson procedure was reported by Nikula (2005), who observed Finnish

EFL classrooms to examine how the L1 and L2 were used. The study revealed that teachers chose the language according to the types of class activities. For instance, they chose the L1 (Finnish) for grammar instruction as well as for classroom management and discipline, while they switched to the L2 (English) for other activities, such as practicing L2 use in a discussion. In other words, the teachers were switching back and forth between the L1 to L2 according to changing activities and aims. Moreover, such pedagogical code-switching by the teacher became a trigger for students to start a new activity during the lesson. As this example shows, once students understand the rules and reasons for language use, both analytical and experiential activities will be mutually supported through the systematic code-switching between the L1 and L2. Needless to say, the L1 use for some analytical activities can be replaced by the L2 as students advance in proficiency. In addition, students might be able to use the L2 to conduct some of the activities categorized under the "mainly L1 use" in the left column if they go through what Littlewood (2004) calls "(pre-) communicative language practices," such as practicing basic expressions or the style of L2 discussion within a structured setting as a preparation. As discussed above, such systematic use of the L1 will provide not only a firm basis of L2 use during the lesson but also bring the point of each activity into focus for students.

3. Language use adapted for proficiency levels and circumstances of the lesson

For the efficient language use during the L2 lesson, it is also crucial to consider students' proficiency levels and the circumstances of the lesson. In order to specify the circumstances, the researcher will refer to the following three categories that reflect the content of the Literature Review and the results of current study:

■ eight circumstances of L2 reading lesson examined by the post-research questionnaire (PRSQ), which are when the teacher is explaining vocabulary, when the teacher is explaining grammar rules and structures, when the teacher is providing answers to reading comprehension tests (RCTs), when the teacher is explaining answer of RCTs, when the teacher is asking questions, when the teacher is making classroom announcements, when students are having a discussion, and when students are answering the questions;

■ four levels of reading adopted from Coté et al. (1998), which are categorized into integrated comprehension, encapsulated comprehension, fragmentary comprehension, or assimilated comprehension according to the quality of the textbase and degree of background knowledge use as described in the Literature Review; and

■ four settings of L2 reading tasks based on Cummins' quadrants (2001), in which the influence of two variables, i.e., contextual clue and cognitive load, are considered as discussed in the Literature Review.

In order to illustrate how language use correlates with university students' proficiency levels and with the circumstances described above during the reading lesson, the researcher designed Figure 20 on the following page.

As Figure 20 shows, students' proficiency levels and circumstances of the lesson are influential factors in deciding the appropriate language use. Although the model is based on a reading lesson, the basic principle seems applicable to other types of lessons targeting different skills, such as listening, speaking, or writing. Referring back to Littlewood model of twofold focus of L2 learning and teaching (2004), the analytical activities can be categorized in the left side column of Figure 20, while the experiential activities can be placed in the right side column, and the middle column of Figure 20 could be either activity.

Chapter IV Discussion 133

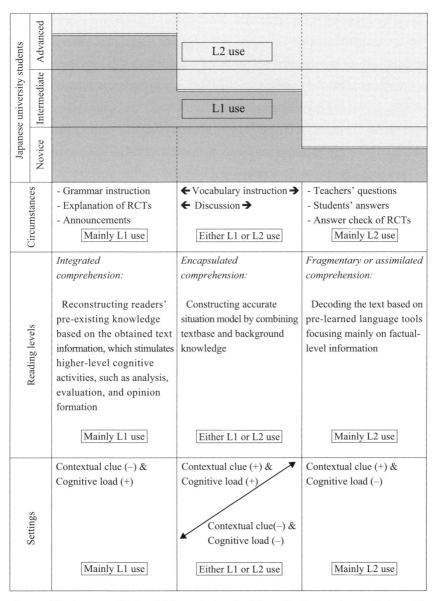

Figure 20. Amount of L1 and L2 use during the L2 reading lesson in association with students' proficiency levels, circumstances of the lesson, reading levels, and settings of reading tasks.

The researcher has deduced pedagogical implications above from the three different perspectives. All of them suggest the flexible and optimal use of the L1 and L2 in order to promote L2 learning. It does not seem rational for teachers and researchers to be trapped by an all-or-nothing argument regarding language use. A more essential task for them is to explore ways to increase L2 use in the classroom without sacrificing students' comprehension or motivation. As discussed in this paper, partial L1 use seems to be one option toward that end. At the same time, if there are other ways to promote L2 learning, they are worth examining as well. For instance, Ushiro (2011) suggested various reading activities so as to maximize students' L2 use and enhance their text comprehension while minimizing the dependence on the L1. He also introduced an effective way of grammar instruction via the L2 in which a new grammar rule is introduced in context so that students can understand the function of the target grammar rule without dealing with difficult L2 terminology (Ushiro, 2014). Once they have learned the rule, students are then provided with ample L2 activities to apply what they have learned in a meaningful setting. These teaching ideas are equally relevant to the issue of effective language use for enhancing L2 learning. What the researcher wants to emphasize is not the dichotomy between the L1 and L2, but the effective ways to use both languages in order to arrive at the best outcome for L2 learning. Therefore, the three models suggested above should be adjusted flexibly according to the individual lesson or classroom situation. The researcher hopes that these models will pave the way for further research and discussion.

C. Limitations

Although the current study has provided important findings regarding the language use during the L2 lesson, there are several limitations that needed to be considered. First, the scale of research might not have been large enough to arrive at an inferential statement based on the results. For instance, the participants were limited in terms of number (N = 87), diversity (focusing on only university students), and their proficiency levels (novice and upper-intermediate levels). The results might vary if a larger number of participants from different age groups, backgrounds, or proficiency levels are examined. Speaking of different backgrounds, second, other differences between the two cohorts (upper-intermediate and novice levels) besides their proficiency levels might have influenced the results of the current study. That is, the upper-intermediate levels consisted of only female participants who were majoring in English literature and international relations, while the novice levels consisted of both male and female participants who were majoring in early childhood or primary education. In addition, each cohort had a different curriculum for English education. Such gender, major, and curricular differences need to be considered in interpreting the results of the current study. Third, the current study has examined only reading comprehension using a single reading text (exposition). If other language skills (e.g., listening, speaking, or writing) are examined, the effects of language use might be different accordingly. Even within the reading research, different genres of text, such as narratives or academic articles, or different topics, whether familiar or unfamiliar might also influence the study results. Fourth, the current study consisted of a single experiment. Therefore, it was not possible to observe how the effects of language use would change along with each individual student's language development. In order to see the relationship between the proficiency level, language use, and its effects on L2 learning within the same student, a longitudinal experiment might be necessary. Finally, the suggested models of L1 and L2 use during the L2 lesson are only applicable for the classroom where the teacher and students share the same L1, such as an EFL classroom in Japan. Obviously, a different approach will be necessary for a multi-lingual classroom. These limitations need to be considered in generalizing the research results to other situations.

D. Future Research

For future research, the researcher will suggest the following three points to be explored further. First, as discussed in the limitation above, other language skills, such as listening, speaking, and writing, need to be examined since different language skills might require different ways of L1 and L2 use. Each language skill can be examined under various circumstances, such as different levels, age groups, purpose of the lesson, or goal of L2 learning. By accumulating the results of individual study, a holistic framework of L1 and L2 use during the L2 lesson will be completed. Considering the current situations of Japanese English education, which strongly promotes exclusive L2 use without any practical guidelines, it is urgent to create such a framework so that individual teachers can refer to and flexibly adapt it for their own teaching environment.

Second, the peer interaction in either the L1 or L2 can be observed more closely in order to examine the effects of language use in detail. Under the current study, the peer interaction in the form of L1 or L2 pair work was analyzed based on the recordings of elicited 16 pairs. Although several interesting findings were indicated within the limited sample, more intensive discourse analysis might be able to reveal how L1 and L2 use will influence a certain situation to facilitate (or hinder) the communication. In addition, different types of pair work also seem worth examining, such as code-switching pair work. If the code-switching pairs show unique patterns of interaction different from L1 or L2 pairs, it could serve as useful information for teachers to identify when and what kind of L1 support is necessary for students to maintain the interaction. Moreover, pairing for peer interaction could be a significant factor to consider. The current study assigned pairs at randomly in order to simulate the authentic classroom situation. Consequently, the differences between participants within a pair — such as more precise proficiency levels or communication styles — were not considered. If a certain pairing would influence the peer interaction itself (see Storch, 2002; Storch & Aldosari, 2012; Watanabe & Swain, 2007), it is worth examining further in association with language use.

Third, from more pedagogical perspective, it will be useful to examine effective ways to code-switch between the L1 and L2 during the lesson. One of the biggest concerns about L1 use during the L2 lesson is that once the L1 is allowed, even partially, students tend to overuse it, and the teacher might lose control over language use. For the sake of efficient L2 learning and teaching, however, it is crucial to maintain the discipline of L1 and L2 use. Therefore, it is important for teachers and researchers to figure out effective ways to control the language use during the lesson. As discussed previously, a suggestion is to explain to students the basic rules and reasons behind the language choice, and to maintain the principle throughout the lesson. Another practical way might be to show visible signs to students at the point of code-switching. For instance, the teacher can display certain symbols of L1 or L2 use, e.g., flags, stickers, or change the classroom format, e.g., standing up during the L2 activities while sitting as a group for L1 discussion. These ideas need to be tested in the actual classroom and developed into more effective strategies.

Chapter V

Conclusion

The current study was designed and conducted in pursuit of the following two goals: to examine the effects of language use during peer interaction in the form of pair work on L2 reading; and to present effective ways to use partial L1 support for promoting L2 learning.

With regard to the first goal, the current study explored whether language use during the pair work would have a significant influence on reading comprehension, as measured by the summary completion test and delayed summary completion test, and on reading attitudes, as measured by the buffer task and post research questionnaire. In relation to these two variables, the current study also examined the influence of English proficiency levels, which in this case were the upper-intermediate and novice levels. The results indicated that different language use during the pair work did not significantly influence students' reading comprehension either for the novice or upper-intermediate level. As for the quality and quantity of pair work production, however, the L1 pair-work groups for both levels outperformed the L2 pair-work groups significantly. Regarding the reading attitudes, it was revealed that the L1 pair-work group at the novice level highly valued the pair work compared to the L2 pair-work group; while the upper-intermediate level did not show such difference between the L1 and L2 pair-work groups. The patterns of pair-work language preference, i.e., L1 preference, L2 preference, or no preference, were significantly different between the L1 and L2 pair-work groups at the upper-intermediate level, while the novice level did not indicate such difference between the groups. Finally, the participants showed different language preference according to different circumstances of the reading lesson. That is, the L1 was preferred significantly more than the L2 in the following three circumstances: when the teacher is explaining grammar rules and structures, when the teacher is explaining the answers of a reading comprehension test, and when the teacher is making classroom announcements. On the other hand, the L2 was preferred significantly more than the L1 in the following two circumstances: when the teacher is providing answers to a reading comprehension test and when the teacher is asking students questions.

The obtained results suggest the following observations:

■ It is possible for the teacher to choose either the L1 or L2 flexibly for pair work to enhance reading comprehension, after carefully considering the level of students and the purpose of a lesson.

■ L1 use is beneficial for the pair work production in terms of quantity and quality regardless of proficiency levels.

■ The novice students tend to appreciate the L1 pair work much more significantly than the L2 pair work.

■ The upper-intermediate level students are linguistically capable of conducting pair work in the L2 if they are encouraged.

■ The appropriate language use will vary according to the circumstances of the reading lesson. That is, L1 use is more suitable when students want to understand precisely the content of the given information, whereas the L2 is preferred when students can expect certain linguistic patterns of interaction that provide opportunities to practice L2 interaction.

Chapter V   Conclusion   *141*

In terms of the second goal, the current study has presented three models of language use, which are associated with (a) a twofold focus of L2 learning and teaching, (b) the process of L2 lesson, and (c) students' proficiency level and circumstances of the lesson. Each model indicates how and when to use the L1 as a support for enhancing L2 learning. In addition, the current study has suggested a new direction of English teaching in Japan. That is, Japanese EFL classrooms in general should aim to raise a "good L2 user" who has appropriate intercultural competence. In addition, acquiring decent knowledge of a specialized field at the university level seems crucial to enrich the content of communication. In order to meet the needs from expanding global society, students need to cultivate their intelligibility and to obtain meaningful content to convey through the communication. For these purposes as well students' L1 can be utilized in various ways. As an overview, Cummins (2007) described the possible contribution of the L1 to L2 learning as follows:

> When students' L1 is invoked as a cognitive and linguistic resource through bilingual instructional strategies, it can function as a stepping stone to scaffold more accomplished performance in the L2. (p.238)

Instead of eliminating students' L1 from the L2 classroom regardless of students' proficiency level or the content of a lesson, it seems more rational to make use of the L1 to support L2 learning since both languages exist in a student's mind and are closely interconnected. As discussed in this paper, the L1 can be helpful in learning about the language as well as acquiring and sharing content-related knowledge in depth. At the same time, L2 use needs to be encouraged for students to experience it in a meaningful context. It is indispensable to have those two types of activities during a lesson, and up to a certain proficiency level, the L1 seems to play an important role to link and facilitate these activities. In order to find a way to pedagogically and affectively support students' L2 learning, further research on effective language use, in either the L1 or L2, in the L2 classroom needs to be conducted.

References

Alderson, J. C. (1984). Reading in a foreign language: A reading problem or a language problem? In J. C. Alderson & A. H. Urquhart (Eds.), *Reading in a foreign language* (pp.1 –27). London: Longman.

Antón, M., & DiCamilla, F. (1998). Socio-cognitive functions of L1 collaborative interaction in the L2 classroom. *The Canadian Modern Language Review, 54,* 314–342.

Bransford, J. D., Brown, A. L., & Cocking, R. R. (2000). *How people learn: Brain, mind, experience, and school.* Washington, DC: National Academy Press.

Brooks-Lewis, K. A. (2009). Adult students' perceptions of the incorporation of their L1 in foreign language teaching and learning. *Applied Linguistics, 30,* 216–235.

Brown, H. D. (2000). *Principles of language learning and teaching* (4th ed.). New York: Longman.

Brown, H. D. (2014). *Principles of language learning and teaching* (6th ed.). New York: Pearson Education.

Butzkamm, W. (2003). We only learn language once. The role of the mother tongue in FL classrooms: Death of a dogma. *The Language Learning Journal, 28,* 29–39.

Byram, M., Nichols, A., & Stevens, D. (Eds.). (2001). *Developing intercultural competence in practice.* Clevedon, UK: Multilingual Matters.

Carless, D. (2008). Student use of the mother tongue in the task-based classroom. *ELT Journal, 62,* 331–338.

Carrell, P. L., & Eisterhold, J. C. (1983). Schema theory and ESL reading pedagogy. *TESOL Quarterly, 17,* 553–573.

Carson, E., & Kashihara, H. (2011). Using the L1 in the L2 classroom: From the Students' perspective. In A. Stewart & N. Sonda (Eds.), *JALT 2011 Conference Proceedings* (pp.713 –724). Tokyo: JALT.

Celce-Murcia, M. (2014). An overview of language teaching methods and approaches. In M. Celce-Murcia, D. M. Brinton, & M. A. Snow (Eds.), *Teaching English as a second or foreign language (4th ed.)* (pp.2–14). Boston, MA: National Geographic Learning.

Clarke, M. (1980). The short circuit hypothesis of ESL reading: Or when language competence interferes with reading performance. *Modern Language Journal, 64,* 203–209.

Cobb, T. (n.d.). *Web VP Classic, v. 4* [computer program]. Retrieved from: www.lextutor.ca/vp/eng/

Cook, G. (2010). *Translation in language teaching.* Oxford, UK: Oxford University Press.

Cook, V. (1999). Going beyond the native speaker in language teaching. *TESOL Quarterly, 35,* 185–209.

Cook, V. (2001). Using the first language in the classroom. *The Canadian Modern Language Review, 57,* 402–423.

Cook, V. (Ed.) (2002). *Portraits of the L2 user.* Clevedon, UK: Multilingual Matters.

Cook, V. (Ed.) (2003). Effects of the second language on the first. Clevedon, UK: Multilingual Matters.

Cook, V. (2004). Bilingual cognition and language teaching. Retrieved from http://homepage.ntlworld.com/vivian.c/Writings/Papers/BilCog&Teaching.htm

Cook, V. (2008). *Second language learning and language teaching* (4th ed.). New York: Routledge.

Cook, V. (2010a). The relationship between first and second language acquisition. In E. Macaro (Ed.), *The continuum comparison to second language acquisition* (pp.137–157). London: Continuum.

Cook, V. (2010b). Questioning traditional assumptions of language teaching. Retrieved from http://homepage.ntlworld.com/vivian.c/Writings/Papers/TradAssumptions.htm

Cook, V. (2011). Consequences of the multi-competence perspective for second language acquisition.
Retrieved from http://homepage.ntlworld.com/vivian.c/Writings/Papers/ConseqB.html

Cook, V. (2013). What are the goals of language teaching? *Iranian Journal of Language Teaching Research, 1,* 44–56.

Cook, V., & Bassettie, B. (Eds.). (2011). *Language and bilingual cognition.* New York: Psychology Press.

Cook, V., Iarossi, E., Stellakis, N., & Tokumaru, Y. (2003). Effects of the L2 on the syntactic processing of the L1. In V. Cook (Ed.), *Effects of the second language on the first* (pp.193–213). Clevedon, UK: Multilingual Matters.

Coté, N., Goldman, S.R., & Saul, E.U. (1998). Students making sense of informational text: Relations between processing and representation. *Discourse Processes, 25,* 1–53.

Council for the Implementation of Education Rebuilding. (2013). University education and global human resource development for the future (3rd proposal). Retrieved from https://www.kantei.go.jp/jp/singi/kyouikusaisei/pdf/dai3_en.pdf

Cromley, J. (2000). *Learning to think, learning to learn: What the science of thinking and learning has to offer adult education.* Washington, D. C.: National Institute for Literacy. Retrieved from http://literacynet.org/lincs/resources/cromley_report.pdf

Cummins, J. (1984). *Bilingualism and special education: Issues in assessment and pedagogy.* Clevedon, UK: Multilingual Matters.

Cummins, J. (2001). *Negotiating identities: Education for empowering in a diverse society* (2nd ed.). Los Angeles: California Association for Bilingual Education.

Cummins, J. (2007). Rethinking monolingual instructional strategies in multilingual classrooms. *Canadian Journal of Applied Linguistics, 10,* 221–240.

Ellis, R. & Shintani, N. (2014). *Exploring language pedagogy through second language acquisition research.* New York: Routledge.

Frawley, W. (1997). Vygotsky and cognitive science: Language and the unification of the social and computational mind. Cambridge, MA: Harvard University Press.

Goodman, K. S. (1967). Reading: A psycholinguistic guessing game. *Journal of the Reading Specialist, 6,* 126–135.

Grabe, W. (2009). *Reading in a second language: Moving from theory to practice.* New York: Cambridge University Press.

Graddol, D. (2006). *English Next.* British Council. Retrieved from http://www.britishcouncil.org/learning-research-englishnext.htm

Hall, G., & Cook, G. (2013). Own-language use in ELT: Exploring global practices and attitudes. *ELT Research Papers, 13*(1). Retrieved from: http://englishagenda.britishcouncil.org/sites/ec/files/C448%20Own%20Language%20use %20in%20ELTA4_FINAL_WEB%20ONLY.pdf

Harmer, J. (2001). *The Practice of English language teaching* (3rd ed.). Harlow, UK: Longman.

Ho, W. K. & Wong, R. Y. L. (Eds.). (2004). *English language teaching in East Asia today.* Singapore: Eastern Universities Press.

Horiba, Y. (1996). Comprehension processes in L2 reading: Language competence, textual coherence, and inferences. *Studies in Second Language Acquisition, 18,* 433–473.

Howatt, A. P. R. (2004). *A history of English language teaching* (2nd ed.). Oxford, UK: Oxford University Press.

Jenkins, J. (2000). *The phonology of English as an international language.* Oxford, UK:

Oxford University Press.

Jenkins, J. (2002). A sociolinguistically based, empirically researched pronunciation syllabus for English as an international language. *Applied Linguistics, 23,* 83–103.

Jenkins, J. (2007). *English as a lingua franca: Attitude and identity.* Oxford, UK: Oxford University Press.

Just, M. A., & Carpenter, P. A. (1992). A capacity theory of comprehension: Individual differences in working memory. *Psychological Review, 99,* 122–149.

Kern, R. G. (1994). The role of mental translation in second language reading. *Studies in Second Language Acquisition, 16,* 441–461.

Kintsch, W. (1988). The role of knowledge in discourse comprehension: A construction-integration model. *Psychological Review, 95,* 163–182.

Kintsch, W. (1998). *Comprehension: A paradigm for cognition.* Cambridge, UK: Cambridge University Press.

Kintsch, W. (2009). Learning and Constructivism. In S. Tobias & T. M. Duffy (Eds.), *Constructivist instruction: Success or failure?* (pp.223–241). New York: Routledge.

Klinger, J. K., & Vaughn, S. (2000). The helping behaviors of fifth graders while using collaborative strategic reading during ESL content classes. *TESOL Quarterly, 34,* 69–98.

Krashen, S. D., & Terrell, T. D. (1983). *The natural approach: Language acquisition in the classroom.* London: Prentice Hall Europe.

Kroll, J. F., & Steward, E. (1994). Category inference in translation and picture naming: Evidence for asymmetric connections between bilingual memory representations. *Journal of Memory and Language, 33,* 149–174.

Lantolf, J. P. (2000). Second language learning as a mediated process. *Language and Applied Linguistics, 33,* 79–96.

Lantolf, J. P., & Thorne, S. L. (2006). Sociocultural theory and second language learning. In B. VanPatten & J. Williams (Eds.), *Theories in second language acquisition: An introduction* (pp. 197–221). New York: Routledge.

Lehti-Eklund, H. (2013). Code-switching to first language in repair: A resource for students' problem solving in a foreign language classroom. *The Journal of International Bilingualism, 17,* 132–152.

Liebscher, G., & Dailey-O'Cain, J. (2005). Student code-switching in the content-based foreign language classroom. *The Modern Language Journal, 89,* 234–247.

Littlewood, W. (2004). The task-based approach: Some questions and suggestions. *ELT*

Journal, 58, 319–326.

Littlewood, W. (2013). Developing a context-sensitive pedagogy for communication-oriented language teaching. *English Teaching, 68,* 3–25.

Littlewood, W. (2014). Communication-oriented language teaching: Where are we now? Where do we go from here? *Language Teaching, 47,* 349–362.

Long, M. (1983). Native speaker/non-native speaker conversation and the negotiation of comprehensible input. *Applied Linguistics, 4,* 126–141.

Long, M. (1996). The role of the linguistic environment in second language acquisition. In W. Ritchie & T. Bhatia (Eds.), *Handbook of second language acquisition* (pp.413–468). San Diego, CA: Academic Press.

Lyster, R. (2014, August 20). *Integrating language and content through counterbalanced instruction.* Address at the 41st JACET summer seminar, Kusatsu sky land hotel, Kusatsu, Gunma.

Macaro, E. (2005). Codeswitching in the L1 classroom: A communication and learning strategy. In E. Llurda (Ed.), *Non-native language teachers: Perceptions, challenges, and contributions to the profession* (pp.63–84). New York: Springer.

Macaro, E., Nakatani, Y. Hayashi, Y., & Khabbazbashi, N. (2012). Exploring the value of bilingual language assistants with Japanese English as a foreign language students. *The Language Learning Journal, 1*–14.

Matsumoto, Y. (2013). The effects of L1/L2 pre-reading activities on reading comprehension and reading attitudes. Unpublished thesis, Graduate Program in English and Cultural Studies, Tsuda College, Tokyo, Japan.

MEXT (2009). Educational guidelines for high school: Foreign language/English. Retrieved from
http://www.mext.go.jp/component/a_menu/education/micro_detail/__icsFiles/afieldfile/2 010/01/29/1282000_9.pdf

MEXT (2013). The English education reform plan responding to the rapid globalization. Retrieved from
http://www.mext.go.jp/a_menu/kokusai/gaikokugo/__icsFiles/afieldfile/2014/01/31/1343 704_01.pdf

MEXT (2014). The results of the 2014 fiscal year English education implementation status survey. Retrieved from
http://www.mext.go.jp/component/a_menu/education/detail/__icsFiles/afieldfile/2015/06/

04/1358566_06_1.pdf

MEXT (2015). Report on the reform of educational content in university 2015 fiscal year. Retrieved from http://www.mext.go.jp/a_menu/koutou/daigaku/04052801/__icsFiles/afieldfile/2016/05/1 2/1361916_1.pdf

MEXT (2015). Survey results on English proficiency level of third-year senior high school students. Retrieved from http://www.mext.go.jp/b_menu/shingi/chousa/shotou/117/shiryo/__icsFiles/afieldfile/201 6/05/24/1368985_7_1.pdf

Mizumoto, A., & Takeuchi, O. (2008). Basics and consideration for reporting effect sizes in research papers. *Eigo Kyoiku KenKyu [Studies of English Education], 31,* 57–66.

Nassaji, H. (2002). Schema theory and knowledge-based processes in second language reading comprehension: A need for alternative perspectives. *Language Learning, 52,* 439–481.

Nikula, T. (2005). English as an object and tool of study in classrooms: Interactional effects and pragmatic implications. *Linguistics and Education, 16,* 27–58.

Ohta, A. (1995). Applying sociocultural theory to an analysis of student discourse: Student-student collaborative interaction in the zone of proximal development. *Issues in Applied Linguistics, 6,* 93–121.

Pickering, L. (2006). Current research on intelligibility in English as a lingua franca. *Annual Review of Applied Linguistics, 26,* 219–233.

Rawson, K. A., & Kintsch, W. (2004). Exploring encoding and retrieval effects of background information on text memory. *Discourse Processes, 38,* 323–344.

Scharauf, R.W., Pavlenko, A., & Dewaele, J-M. (2003). Bilingual episodic memory: An introduction. *The International Journal of Bilingualism, 7,* 2–13.

Scott, V. M., & De La Fuente, M. J. (2008). What's the problem? L2 students' use of the L1 during conscious-raising, form-focused tasks. *The Modern Language Journal, 92,* 100–113.

Seidlhofer, B. (2011). Understanding English as a lingua franca. Oxford, UK: Oxford University Press.

Storch, N. (2002). Patterns of interaction in ESL pair work. *Language Learning, 5,* 119–158.

Storch, N., & Aldosari, A. (2012). Pairing students in pair work activity. *Language Teaching*

Research, 17, 31–48.

Storch, N., & Wigglesworth, G. (2003). Is there a role for the use of the L1 in an L2 setting? *TESOL Quarterly, 37,* 760–770.

Swain, M. (1985). Communicative competence: some roles of comprehensible input and comprehensible output in its development. In S. Gass and C. Madden (Eds.), *Input in Second Language Acquisition* (pp.235–256). Rowley, MA: Newbury House.

Swain, M. (2006). Languaging, agency and collaboration in advanced second language learning. In H. Byrnes (Ed.), *Advanced Language Learning: The Contributions of Halliday and Vygotsky.* London: Continuum.

Swain, M., Brooks, L., & Tocalli-Beller, A. (2002). Peer-peer dialogue as a means of second language learning. *Annual Review of Applied Linguistics, 22,* 171–185.

Swain, M., & Lapkin, S. (1998). Interaction and second language learning: Two adolescent French immersion students working together. *The Modern Language Journal, 82,* 320–337.

Swain, M., & Lapkin, S. (2000). Task-based second language learning: The uses of the first language. *Language Teaching Research, 4,* 251–274.

Sweetnam Evans, M. (2011). Reading bilinguals reading: First language use and comprehension monitoring in the reading of different textual genres. *New Zealand Studies in Applied Linguistics, 17,* 53–69.

Taylor, L. (2013) Testing reading through summary: Investigating summary completion tasks for assessing reading comprehension ability. Cambridge, UK: Cambridge University.

Tian, L., & Macaro, E. (2012). Comparing the effect of teacher codeswitching with English-only explanations on the vocabulary acquisition of Chinese university students: A Lexical focus-on-form study. *Language Teaching Research, 16,* 367–391.

Upton, T., & Lee-Thompson, L-C. (2001). The role of the first language in second language reading. *SSLA, 23,* 469–495.

Ushiro, Y. (Ed.). (2009). *Eigo Reading no Kagaku: Yometa-tsumori no nazo wo toku* [Science of Reading in English: To reveal the secret of reading]. Tokyo: Ken-kyu-sha.

Ushiro, Y. (Ed.). (2011). *Eigo de Eigo o Yomu Jugyo* [Lessons of Reading English in English]. Tokyo: Ken-kyu-sha.

Ushiro, Y (Ed.). (2014). Eigo de Oshieru Ei-bun-po [Teaching Grammar in Context]. Tokyo: Ken-kyu-sha.

Van den Branden, K. (2000). Does negotiation of meaning promote reading comprehension? A study of multilingual primary school classes. *Reading Research Quarterly, 35,* 426–443.

van Dijk, T.A., & Kintsch, W. (1983). *Strategies of discourse comprehension.* New York: Academic Press.

Vygotsky, L. (1997). Interaction between learning and development. In M. Gauvain, & M. Cole (Eds.), *Readings on the development of children* (pp.79–91). New York: W. H. Freeman and Company. (Reprinted from *Mind in Society,* 1978, Cambridge, MA: Harvard University Press).

Watanabe, Y., & Swain, M. (2007). Effects of proficiency differences and patterns of pair interaction on second language learning: collaborative dialogue between adult ESL students. *Language Teaching Research, 11,* 121–142.

Wolter, B. (2006). Lexical network structures and L2 vocabulary acquisition: The role of L1 lexical/conceptual knowledge. *Applied Linguistics, 27,* 741–747.

Yamashita, J. (2001). Transfer of L1 reading ability to L2 reading: An elaboration of the linguistic threshold. Studies in Language and Culture, *23,* 189–200. Nagoya, Japan: Graduate School of Language and Culture, Nagoya University.

Yen-Chi, F. (2009). Implementing collaborative strategic reading (CSR) in an EFL context in Taiwan. Unpublished doctoral dissertation, University of Leicester, UK. Retrieved from

https://lra.le.ac.uk/bitstream/2381/7555/1/Yen-Chi%20Fan's%20final%20submission.pdf

Appendix A
Previous Research

The participants of the previous research (Matsumoto, 2013) were 56 Japanese university students (freshmen and sophomores: 29 men and 27 women), and their English proficiency level was roughly the intermediate level (Mean of TOEFL PBT = 488.43, SD = 33.09). The participants were divided into two groups randomly, and each group engaged in pre-reading activities (PRAs) either in L1 (n = 32) or in L2 (n = 24). There was no significant difference between the groups in terms of their English proficiency according to the TOEFL scores, $t(54) = .72, p > .47$.

Three instruments of data collection were employed: (1) reading comprehension tests (RCTs: 10 multiple-choice questions in English) and summary writing tasks (SWTs: filling in 10 blanks with Japanese words or phrases to complete a Japanese summary of the reading text); (2) post-reading questionnaires (PRDQs: four multiple-choice questions regarding participants' evaluation of PRAs in relation to RCT and SWT and the reasons for their evaluation), (3) a post-research questionnaire (PRSQ: three multiple-choice questions regarding the relationship between the PRAs and reading attitudes, such as motivation, comprehension, and reading anxiety; participants' evaluation of language use during the PRAs; and their language preference for eight different occasions during the reading lesson).

The data were collected twice, at a four-week interval, using two types of expositional texts: one was on a familiar topic (E1: university students' cheating on the SAT) and the other was about an unfamiliar topic (E2: the last cycad tree in the world). The procedures of data collection were: (1) small-group pre-reading activities (PRAs: including "listing, ordering, ranking, and mapping) conducted in L1-PRA group and L2-PRA group; (2) individual reading (E1 text); (3) reading comprehension test (RCT); (4) summary writing test (SWT); (5) post-reading questionnaire (PRQ). For the second data collection after a four-week interval, the same procedures were repeated using the E2 text, and the post-research questionnaire (PRSQ) was conducted at the end. The procedure of the experiment is summarized as follows:

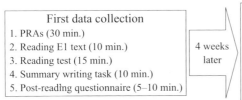

Appendix B
Informed Consent

英語リーディングに関するリサーチへのご協力のお願い

　本研究の目的は、英語リーディングのプロセスを明らかにすることです。

　リサーチャーが研究の内容を説明し参加者の同意を得たうえで、研究に参加していただくことになります。所要時間は約70分の予定です。本研究に参加するかどうかは参加者の自由です。参加を断ったとしても何ら不利益を受けることはありません。

　また本研究を通じて得られた情報は、貴重な研究成果として学術団体の総会や学術雑誌などで発表されることがあります。しかしいずれの場合も、参加者の名前や個人が特定される情報は一切公開されません。プライバシー保護には最善の配慮をいたします。

　本研究に関して更に詳しいことを知りたい場合はリサーチャーまでご連絡ください。

リサーチャー　津田塾大学文学研究科後期博士課程　松本祐子

連絡先：xxxxxxxx@gm.tsuda.ac.jp

アドバイザー　津田塾大学英文学科教授　田近裕子

連絡先：xxxxxxxx@tsuda.ac.jp

同　意　書

津田塾大学文学研究科　松本祐子 殿

研究課題名「英語リーディングに関する研究」

　上記研究課題の内容についてリサーチャーより説明を受け、その内容を十分理解しましたので研究に参加することに同意し以下に署名します。

氏　名 _____

同意年月日 _____　年　　　　月　　　　日

Appendix C
Taylor's Research on Reading Summary

According to Taylor (2013), reading comprehension means constructing a mental representation of the text, and it can be assessed via summary tasks (p.56). That is because summary tasks require readers to use "higher order reading skills," such as identifying essential information, figuring out the hierarchical structure of text segments, and discarding unnecessary information (p.60). If readers can demonstrate such higher reading skills through a summary task, their reading comprehension skills will be recognized as well. Among different types of summary tasks, Taylor considers a summary completion task as one of the most appropriate measurements of reading comprehension for the following reasons: (a) has little influence from language production skills, (b) has little influence from previous summary instruction or readers' level of maturity, and (c) is convenient for grading purposes (p.80). Therefore, her research aimed to create a summary completion task that would assess reading comprehension accurately based on a wide range of data collection.

For the purpose above, Taylor examined students' oral and written recall of L1 reading texts. Her research consisted of three phases:

1. Having 40 advanced-level students (aged 16–18) recall the L1 texts orally to elicit their mental representations of texts that were then statistically analyzed according to which propositions tended to be recalled more frequently or more easily.

2. Having 82 mixed-level students (age 14–15) do written recalls on the same texts in order to examine which propositions were salient for both strong and weak readers and which propositions were difficult for

less skilled readers to obtain in their written summary.

3. Based on the analysis of oral and written recalls, a model summary of each text and text-removed summary completion task was created. These summary completion tasks were tested on 170 mixed-level students (age 13–14). The students were asked to provide written responses to fill in 39 blanks in the sample summary.

The results of the research indicated a high level of test reliability for assessing reading comprehension. Further description and analysis of the results can be found in Taylor's research (2013, pp. 83–205).

Appendix D
Reading Text

以下は「拒食症」に関する新聞記事です。このテキストに関するタスクを後で行ってもらいますので、内容をしっかり理解できるよう丁寧に読んでください。

なお二重線の語彙は必要があれば語彙リストを参照してください。

The rights and wrongs of treating anorexia

The case of Samantha Kendall, the anorexia nervosa sufferer who discharged herself from hospital despite doctors' fears for her life, has highlighted the confusion in public thinking about this disturbing and perplexing disease.

Ten years ago anorexia was still dismissed as nothing more than slimming gone too far.

Today it is recognized as a treatable medical condition; but the degree to which treatment should be carried out without the patient's consent has become a topic of debate.

Researchers have suggested two psychiatric explanations behind the onset of anorexia.

One is that the patient, faced with an unacceptably stressful or difficult adult life, is trying to retreat into childhood or avoid leaving it.

Another is that choosing what to eat – and specifically choosing not to eat - is often an attempt to exert control by people who feel that their lives are too constrained in other ways.

But the truth is that for all the resources that have been devoted to its study, the syndrome remains imperfectly understood.

It is beyond doubt, however, that anorexia is a severe psychiatric disorder. There is no other way to describe an illness that allows a patient to look in the mirror at her own emaciated, starved body, and see someone obese staring back.

Severe sufferers often deny that they are trying to kill themselves, but the diet they are pursuing is all too likely to make death inevitable.

The 1983 Mental Health Act provides for sufferers from severe psychiatric disorders to be held in hospital for treatment against their will if there is a danger that they will do harm to themselves or others.

Yet even thought one in 10 anorexia sufferers dies, doctors are sometimes reluctant to use their powers under the law.

This is often because of a fear that treatment by compulsion is self-defeating, since forced-fed victims of anorexia often return to starvation diets when they get home.

There is clearly work to be done in making the treatment of extreme anorexia – which often involves leaving patients in isolation and without their clothes, and watching them as they eat and go to the lavatory – more humane.

But the shortcomings of the available treatments should not obscure the fact that the alternative to treatment can sometimes be death.

If doctors made more use of the powers available to them, lives could be saved.

語彙	英語の意味	日本語の意味
anorexia (nervosa)	an eating disorder that makes people lose more weight than is considered healthy for their age and height	神経性無食欲症・拒食症
discharge	send somebody away	解放する・退院させる
perplexing	confusing	ややこしい
psychiatric	relating to the study or treatment of mental illness	精神（医学）の
onset	the beginning of something	徴候・発病
retreat	moving back	後退・退行
exert	to use one's power	力などを用いる
emaciated	extremely thin	やせ衰えた
starved	extremely hungry	飢えた
obese	extremely fat	肥満の
staring	to look fixedly at something	じっと見ている
compulsion	by force	強制
lavatory	bathroom, restroom	トイレ
humane	having a concern for the suffering of another	人道的な
shortcoming(s)	negative point	欠点
obscure	to make unclear	不明瞭にする

Appendices *159*

Appendix E
Summary Completion Test

以下は先ほど読んだテキスト（*The rights and wrongs of treating anorexia*）のサマリーです。

それぞれの括弧に入る最も適切な解答を解答用紙の選択肢から選び、その解答に丸をつけて下さい。問題は全部で21問あります。

A recent news case has raised an important issue concerning anorexia.

A girl suffering from anorexia (1) hospital against her doctor's advice.

Changing attitudes

Although anorexia used to be regarded as a (2), it is now generally accepted as a (3). The current issue is whether anorexia sufferers should be treated without their (4).

Understanding the disease

Different explanations have been offered for anorexia. Sufferers may want to (5) childhood since they (6) the pressures of adult life. Alternatively, people who feel their lives are (7) may choose what or what not to eat because it gives them a feeling of being (8). Our understanding of the disease, despite extensive research, is (9).

The nature of the disease

It is clear that anorexia is a serious (10) disorder. Otherwise extreme sufferers would not be able to see themselves in (11) and see someone

160

(12). Severe anorexia can lead to death although sufferers generally believe they are not trying to (13).

Treating anorexia

The (14) of 1983 makes it possible to force treatment on sufferers.

Although one in ten sufferers (15), doctors are often reluctant to use (16) because they think the treatment will be (17) in the long run.

The way ahead

New ways of treating extreme anorexia are needed. Current methods – such as leaving patients (18) and watching them (19) – could be described as (20). It may be the case, however, that such treatment is (21) if the alternative is to die.

1	a) went to	b) worked for	c) checked out	d) stayed in
2	a) mental problem	b) dieting problem	c) educational problem	d) social problem
3	a) untreatable illness	b) minor problem	c) eating habit	d) curable disease
4	a) payment	b) approval	c) support	d) food
5	a) forget about	b) remember	c) go back to	d) escape from
6	a) do not have	b) do not worry about	c) cannot accept	d) cannot imagine
7	a) organized	b) exciting	c) controlled	d) happy
8	a) dependent	b) independent	c) fat	d) slim
9	a) no use	b) limited	c) satisfying	d) clear
10	a) mental	b) physical	c) genetic	d) brain
11	a) the bed	b) the restaurant	c) the hospital	d) the mirror
12	a) slim	b) short	c) fat	d) tall
13	a) feed themselves	b) kill themselves	c) improve themselves	d) encourage themselves

14	a) insurance policy	b) patients' organization	c) mental health act	d) doctors' conference
15	a) can be cured	b) can be hospitalized	c) can die	d) can eat
16	a) their power	b) their skill	c) their facility	d) their money
17	a) suitable	b) useless	c) expensive	d) painful
18	a) with a nurse	b) with a doctor	c) by themselves	d) among other patients
19	a) eat and use the bathroom	b) eat and sleep	c) eat and take a shower	d) eat and exercise
20	a) ineffective	b) inexpensive	c) inconvenient	d) inhumane
21	a) popular	b) necessary	c) cruel	d) useless

Name [   ]

Appendix F
Delayed Summary Completion Test

以下は先日読んだテキスト（*The rights and wrongs of treating anorexia*）のサマリーです。読んだ内容を思い出しながらそれぞれの括弧に入る最も適切な解答を解答用紙の選択肢から選び、その解答に丸をつけて下さい。

問題は全部で 21 問あります。

A recent news case has raised an important issue concerning anorexia.

A girl suffering from anorexia (1) hospital against her doctor's advice.

Changing attitudes

Although anorexia used to be regarded as a (2), it is now generally accepted as a (3). The current issue is whether anorexia sufferers should be treated without their (4).

Understanding the disease

Different explanations have been offered for anorexia. Sufferers may want to (5) childhood since they (6) the pressures of adult life. Alternatively, people who feel their lives are (7) may choose what or what not to eat because it gives them a feeling of being (8). Our understanding of the disease, despite extensive research, is (9).

The nature of the disease

It is clear that anorexia is a serious (10) disorder. Otherwise extreme sufferers would not be able to see themselves in (11) and see someone

(12). Severe anorexia can lead to death although sufferers generally believe they are not trying to (13).

Treating anorexia

The (14) of 1983 makes it possible to force treatment on sufferers.

Although one in ten sufferers (15), doctors are often reluctant to use (16) because they think the treatment will be (17) in the long run.

The way ahead

New ways of treating extreme anorexia are needed. Current methods – such as leaving patients (18) and watching them (19) – could be described as (20). It may be the case, however, that such treatment is (21) if the alternative is to die.

1	a) went to	b) worked for	c) checked out	d) stayed in
2	a) mental problem	b) dieting problem	c) educational problem	d) social problem
3	a) untreatable illness	b) minor problem	c) eating habit	d) curable disease
4	a) payment	b) approval	c) support	d) food
5	a) forget about	b) remember	c) go back to	d) escape from
6	a) do not have	b) do not worry about	c) cannot accept	d) cannot imagine
7	a) organized	b) exciting	c) controlled	d) happy
8	a) dependent	b) independent	c) fat	d) slim
9	a) no use	b) limited	c) satisfying	d) clear
10	a) mental	b) physical	c) genetic	d) brain
11	a) the bed	b) the restaurant	c) the hospital	d) the mirror
12	a) slim	b) short	c) fat	d) tall
13	a) feed themselves	b) kill themselves	c) improve themselves	d) encourage themselves

14	a) insurance policy	b) patients' organization	c) mental health act	d) doctors' conference
15	a) can be cured	b) can be hospitalized	c) can die	d) can eat
16	a) their power	b) their skill	c) their facility	d) their money
17	a) suitable	b) useless	c) expensive	d) painful
18	a) with a nurse	b) with a doctor	c) by themselves	d) among other patients
19	a) eat and use the bathroom	b) eat and sleep	c) eat and take a shower	d) eat and exercise
20	a) ineffective	b) inexpensive	c) inconvenient	d) inhumane
21	a) popular	b) necessary	c) cruel	d) useless

Name [   ]

Appendix G
Buffer Task

以下の情報を日本語で記入してください。

(1) あなたの名前：_____

(2) あなたの所属学科と学年：_____学科　____年

(3) 一番最近受験した TOEFL スコアと受験時期：____点____年____月

(4) 英語圏に留学・居住経験のある方に聞きます：

滞在場所_____（例：アメリカ、ニュージーランド、シンガポール等）

滞在期間_____（例：3歳から10歳、2000年から2005年等）

所属教育機関_____

（例：現地小学校、インターナショナル・スクール、日本人学校等）

(5) 先ほど読んだテキストの感想を以下5つの選択肢の中から選んで○を付けてください。

a. 難しかった

b. やや難しかった

c. どちらとも言えない

d. やや易しかった

e. 易しかった

(6) 先ほど読んだテキストのトピックについて以前読んだり聞いたりして：

a. よく知っていた

b. 少し知っていた

c. どちらとも言えない

d. ほとんど知らなかった

e. 全く知らなかった

質問は以上です。

なお提供して頂いた個人情報は学術研究の目的以外には一切使用しません。

ご協力ありがとうございました。

166

Appendix H
Pair Work Focus Questions

■ L1 pair work

以下の質問（1 – 7 番）についてパートナーと話し合い、話し合った内容を出来るだけ詳しく日本語で記録して下さい。質問ごとに時間を区切って行いますので指示があるまで

次の頁に進まないで下さい。

氏名：	パートナーの氏名：

1. 記事では Samantha Kendall という人についてどのような事が書かれていましたか？

Appendices　*167*

2. Anorexia への見方が 10 年前と現在ではどのように変化したと書かれていましたか？

（10 年前）

（現在）

3. Anorexia が発症する原因だと推測される 2 つの要因はどんなものですか？
（要因 1 ）

（要因 2 ）

168

4. 重症の Anorexia 患者が自分自身をどのように認識して（見て）いるかについてどんな事例が挙げられていましたか？

5. Anorexia 患者への対応について 1983 年の法律はどのように定めていますか？
また医師は実際それらの患者にどのように対応していますか？
その理由は何ですか？

（1983 年の法律）：

（医師の実際の対応とその理由）：

Appendices *169*

6. 重症の Anorexia 患者にどのように対応すべきだと作者は述べています
か？

7．記事のタイトルを覚えていますか？

質問は以上です。

170

■ L2 pair work

Discuss the following questions (#1-7) and write down what you & your partner talked about each question. Try to write as much as possible *in English* without worrying about grammar/spelling mistakes.

Please do not look at the next page until you are told to do so.

Your name:	Your parter's name:

1. Can you recall anything in the editorial about a person called Samantha Kendall?

Appendices *171*

2. Can you recall anything in the editorial about how people's perspectives on anorexia have changed for the last ten years?

Ten years ago:

Today:

3. Can you recall two possible causes for anorexia described in the editorial?

1st cause:

2nd cause:

172

4. Can you recall any example of how anorexia patients perceive (see) themselves?

5. Can you recall anything about the 1983 Mental Health Act establishing the treatment of severe anorexia sufferers?

Also, can you recall how doctors *actually* treat severe anorexia patients   and why?

Treatment set by the 1983 Mental Health Act:

Actual doctors' treatments and their reasons:

Appendices *173*

6. Can you recall the writer's opinion about how to treat extreme anorexia
   sufferers?

7. Can you recall the title of the editorial?

This is the end of the question.

Appendix I
Answer Key for the Pair Work Focus Questions (FQs)

	L1	L2
FQ1	1. 拒食症患者 2. 医師の心配にも関わらず病院を出てしまった	1. Anorexia sufferer 2. Discharged herself from hospital despite of doctor's concern
FQ 2	1. 単なる痩せすぎの問題で治療対象ではない（又は）食習慣の問題 2. 治療可能な病状（又は）深刻な心理的問題	1. Just-slimming gone too far (or) dieting problem 2. Treatable medical condition (or) psychiatric disorder
FQ 3	1. ストレス・困難に直面した時 2. 子供時代に戻りたい・留まりたいと考えること 3. 他人からコントロールされていると感じる場合 4. 何を食べるかを自分で決定することでコントロールを取り戻したいと考えること	1. In facing stress/difficulty 2. People want to retreat into childhood or to avoid leaving it 3. In feeling one's life is controlled by others, 4. Trying to regain own control by choosing what to eat
FQ 4	1. 本当はやせ細っているのに 2. 自分を太っているとみなす	1. Perceiving their skinny bodies 2. As being fat
FQ 5	1. 深刻な場合は医師による強制的治療も許可されている 2. 法が許可した強制的治療をためらう場合が多い 3. 退院してしまえば元に戻り効果がないことを知っているから	1. If necessary, forced-treatment is allowed by doctor 2. Doctors are reluctant to use their power 3. Since it is useless once a patient leaves the hospital
FQ 6	1. 人間的な取り扱いには留意すべきだが 2. 必要であれば患者の命を救うために医者はもっと強制力を使うべき	1. Although patients should be treated in a humane way, 2. If necessary, doctors should use forced-treatment more to save patients' lives.
FQ 7	1. The rights and wrongs 2. of treating 3. anorexia	1. The rights and wrongs 2. of treating 3. anorexia

合計：18 点   Total: 18 points

Appendix J
Post-research Questionnaire

以下の質問に該当する答えに丸をつけてください。

(1) 事前に行ったペアワークはサマリー・タスクをやる時に：

    a.「役に立った」

    b.「どちらかと言えば役に立った」

    c.「どちらかと言えば役に立たなかった」

    d.「役に立たなかった」

(2) 問1で選んだ答えの理由を以下の選択肢から**1つだけ選び**アルファベットに丸をつけてください。該当する項目がない場合は「その他」に理由を記述して下さい。

    →「役に立った」・「どちらかと言えば役に立った」と答えた人：

a. 背景知識を得ることができたから	b. 主題や重要なポイントを理解できたから
c. 細かい部分まで理解できたから	d. 語彙の理解に役立ったから
e. その他〔　　　　　　　　　　　　　　　　　　　　　　　　　　　　　〕	

    →「役に立たなかった」・「どちらかと言えば役に立たなかった」と答えた人：

a. 背景知識を得られなかったから	b. 主題や重要なポイントを理解できなかったから
c. 細かい部分まで理解できなかったから	d. 語彙の理解に役立たなかったから
e. その他〔　　　　　　　　　　　　　　　　　　　　　　　　　　　　　〕	

(3) 今回のレッスンに関してペアワーク中に使う言語は：

    a. 日本語が良い

    b. 英語が良い

    c. 日本語と英語どちらでやっても変わりない

176

(4) 問3で選んだ答えの理由を以下の選択肢から**ひとつだけ選び**アルファベットに丸をつけて下さい。

a	スムーズに意思疎通できペアワークしやすいから。ストレスがたまらないから。
b	単語・表現が分からず説明できないから。苦手だから。
c	細部まで説明できるから。詳細情報まで共有できるから。
d	内容を深く考えられるから。
e	テキストの理解が目的だから。
f	テキストの内容が難しいから。
g	素早く情報交換できるから。
h	考える時間が長くなってしまうから。
i	テキスト（又はサマリー）が英語だから。そのまま利用できるから。
j	テキストの内容を思い出しやすいから。
k	良い練習（機会）になるから。学習に必要だから。
l	その他（どちらでも気にしないから。上手く使える方を使えば良いから。それぞれに良さがあるから。等）

(5) 次は一般的な英語リーディングのクラスに関する質問です。

クラスの中で部分的に使用言語を変えるとしたら、以下8つの場面でそれぞれ**日本語と英語のどちらを使いたいですか？**

どちらかの言語を選び8つの場面全てに関して丸をつけて下さい。

場面	日本語	英語
語彙・表現の説明		
文法・構文の説明		
読解問題の解答		
読解問題の解説		
学生同士のディスカッション		
教師から学生に対する質問		
質問に対する学生からの答え		
宿題やテストに関する連絡事項		

★上記の回答を学術データとして無記名で使用する事を承諾してくださる方は以下に署名をお願いします

［名前：　　　　　　　　　　　　　　　　　　　　　　　　］

＝ご協力ありがとうございました＝

Appendix K
Pilot Study

The participants of the pilot study were intermediate-level Japanese university students (English literature major first-year female students), and they were divided into two groups: one was the L1 pair-work group (n = 20), and the other was the L2 pair-work group (n = 19). According to their TOEFL score, there was no significant difference between L1 pair-work group (Mean = 459.30, SD = 30.44) and L2 pair-work group (Mean = 474.52, SD = 17.04): $t(30) = 1.94$, $p = .06$, Cohen's $d = .61$.

For the pilot study, the same data collection instruments (except the post-research questionnaire, question [4]), experimental procedure, and data analysis tools were adopted, which were described in Chapter 3 (Data collection instruments). After the pilot study, the researcher confirmed that the experimental procedure worked well. There were, however, several points revised based on the results of pilot study in order to improve the experimental tools and procedure. The revised parts are summarized as follows:

■ One of the definitions on the glossary attached to the reading was revised. The original definition of the word, "discharge" was provided as "to release someone from a place where he/she was trapped [Kai-ho suru]." Many of the participants, however, had difficulty in associating the definition with the context of reading (i.e., to discharge an anorexia patient from the hospital). Therefore, the researcher added another definition to the glossary, "to give someone a permission to leave a place, such as a hospital (*Tai'in saseru*)."

■ Pair-work focus questions (2) and (5) were revised in order to make the questions more easily understood. The original question (2): "Can you recall anything in the editorial about how attitudes to anorexia have changed for the last ten years?" was revised into "...how *people's perspective on anorexia* has changed in the last ten years?" In addition, the original question (5): "Can you recall anything mentioned about the current legal position on treating severe anorexia sufferers?" was changed into "... mentioned about *the 1983 Mental Health Act establishing the treatment of* server anorexia sufferers?" (revised expressions are in italics). The same revisions were made for the L1 pair-work focus questions as well.

■ In order to avoid ambiguity, the researcher modified two sections of the original reading text for the summary completion test. One was in the second paragraph, ".... sufferers should be treated without *their* [approval]" and the other was in the fifth paragraph, "The [mental health act] *of 1983* makes it possible to ..." (added expressions are in italics). The purpose of adding these expressions was to provide the readers with more specific information so that they could choose the appropriate answers in brackets for each sentence without being confused by ambiguous expressions.

■ The instructions of post-research questionnaire, question (5) were revised. In order to avoid the confusion, the new instructions specifically pointed out that participants need to choose which language (L1 or L2) they would prefer to use for eight different occasions. Some of the participants in the pilot study misunderstood the instructions and chose only one language for all the occasions. Therefore, this change was made not to lose valuable responses from the participants in the main data collection.

■ Auther

松本　祐子　（Yuko　Matsumoto）

モンタレー国際研究大学院大学（Monterey Institute of International Studies）
英語教育修士課程修了（英語教育修士）、津田塾大学文学研究科コミュニ
ケーション研究英語教育後期博士課程修了（文学博士）。早稲田大学、宮
崎国際大学を経て現在宮崎公立大学で英語教育に携わる。主な研究領域
は、英語教育における学習者の母語活用、読解指導、日本人英語教師の
在り方など。

The Effects of L1 and L2 Use in the L2 Classroom
第二言語指導における学習者母語活用の可能性

2017 年 10 月 10 日　初版第 1 刷発行

■ 著　　　者———松本祐子
■ 発 行 者———佐藤　守
■ 発 行 所———株式会社 **大学教育出版**
　　　　　　　　〒 700-0953　岡山市南区西市 855-4
　　　　　　　　電話（086）244-1268　FAX（086）246-0294
■ 印刷製本———モリモト印刷㈱

ⒸYuko Matsumoto 2017, Printed in Japan
検印省略　　　落丁・乱丁本はお取り替えいたします。
本書のコピー・スキャン・デジタル化等の無断複製は著作権法上での例外を除き禁じられて
います。本書を代行業者等の第三者に依頼してスキャンやデジタル化することは、たとえ個
人や家庭内での利用でも著作権法違反です。

ISBN978 - 4 - 86429 - 467 - 6